THE TAKEOVER OF PUBLIC EDUCATION IN AMERICA

The Agenda to Control Information and Knowledge
Through the Accountability System

A. PATRICK HUFF, PH.D.

authorHOUSE®

AuthorHouse™
1663 Liberty Drive
Bloomington, IN 47403
www.authorhouse.com
Phone: 1 (800) 839-8640

Published by AuthorHouse 03/02/2015

ISBN: 978-1-4969-6860-9 (sc)
ISBN: 978-1-4969-6861-6 (hc)
ISBN: 978-1-4969-6859-3 (e)

Library of Congress Control Number: 2015901867

Print information available on the last page.

Contents

CONTENTS

LIST OF TABLES

Table

To all those in the education profession who work diligently to prepare our current students for the world in which we live, may you find the resolve to move beyond the limitations placed upon you through the system and open the channels of information and knowledge to your students. I would also like to acknowledge those individuals who agreed to share their stories and create a pathway to document this information. Without your assistance, this book would not exist.

To my wife, Connie, and my children, Bobby, Lauren, and Kristin; thank you for your support and encouragement in my pursuit of this endeavor. I love you all.

Foreword

The condition of education today indicates the patient is currently on life support, with drive-by remedies applied without regard to the institutional inequities that persist in every school district in the United States. Teachers, principals, superintendents, parents, and most of all students, are constantly labeled as 'failing' without regard to the lasting connotation of what this implies. Imagine being constantly told that you are a *failure* and that no matter what you do, or what remedies are applied, there will be lasting psycho-social impact as you seek to demonstrate to society that you are no longer a failure.

This is the environment the majority of public school teachers and children seek to teach and learn in under the guise of accountability in today's 21st century model of miseducation. The concept of deficit thinking is not only operational, it guides all of our educational decisions, whether at the state, local or national level. Poor children attend schools without textbooks and fully functional facilities while dedicated teachers attempt to teach without adequate support from the broader community, including district stakeholders. Despite the inequities, however, children continue to attend schools and teachers continue to teach, responding to a higher calling and a more realistic understanding of what teaching and learning should look like.

Dr. Huff's book is riveting in its approach and its content. It clearly delineates the many players in the bifurcation of education dollars; dollars allocated for the purported intended purpose of improving student outcomes. As a former teacher, principal and Assistant Superintendent, I challenge everyone concerned with the future of education to explore and expand upon the hypotheses postulated by Dr. Huff. These hypotheses are grounded in the reality of our innate dedication to the notion that education should be available for every child irrespective of class of familial condition. The very foundation of our education and indeed our democracy depends on it!

Patricia Hoffman-Miller, Associate Professor Educational Leadership – January 28, 2015

Nearly 15 years ago, I was at a meeting at our central office and had the opportunity to hear Dr. Alan Patrick Huff profess his concerns about new initiatives his campus was being asked to implement. These new initiatives were designed to improve student learning, so students could perform better on state exams in order to meet the accountability standards. He spoke with much passion and knowledge, and I was both intrigued and impressed with his desire to make the right decision for his high school campus. At that time, Dr. Huff, was the principal of a 5A high school in a large suburban school district.

Before this meeting, I had never met Dr. Huff, but I knew of his outstanding reputation. As the Associate Principal for Curriculum and Instruction at a high school in the same district with Dr. Huff, I began attending meetings where Dr. Huff was present. I was able to listen to Dr. Huff articulate his thoughts about our educational system and grew to admire his wise perspective.

Dr. Huff has served 34 years in public education. He has held a number of positions including teacher for 4 years, assistant principal for 19 years, and principal of a middle school and high school for 11 years. During this time, he was honored with The Secondary Principal of the Year Award. After retiring as principal of Klein High School, Dr. Huff continued his education by obtaining a doctorate degree in educational leadership while at the same time serving as an adjunct professor at several universities. Currently, he is teaching graduate courses and continuing his research on the accountability system in American public schools.

The book, *The Takeover of Public Education in America: The Agenda to Control Information and Knowledge through the Accountability System*, is a lifetime of work for Dr. Huff. He has taken his many years of experience in public education and coupled it with his research to tell the compelling story of our Nation's education accountability system. He has had a front row seat for 4 decades of federal mandates being asserted on the public schools in the name of improved student achievement.

Dr. Huff spent several years researching this topic and interviewing individuals who were adversely impacted by school closures due to the federal accountability system. His research tells a historical story that is provocative and 'eye opening.' In the end, Dr. Huff challenges educators and citizens to be "…informed and aware so that our actions and decisions when it comes to the education of our youth is just and right."

I highly recommend this book as a must read. You will become more informed about education policy as it pertains to our accountability system; along with reading riveting testimony from individuals who have firsthand knowledge and experience with an alleged failing school district. The reading does not offer an alternative for our educational system. Rather, Dr. Huff presents accurate information so those who want to consider educational reform are better equipped to do so.

Teresa A. Hughes, PhD, adjunct professor and public school consultant

PROLOGUE

In the late fall of 2012, I reached out to members of two communities that were facing major challenges with their schools. One was located on the east side of Austin, Texas, and the other was located in the north sector of Houston. The community in Austin was part of the Austin Independent School District. The community in Houston was part of the North Forest Independent School District. This book is their story. It is the story of the struggle of parents, their children, and the educators whose lives are affected by the mandates of No Child Left Behind. The schools attended by the students, and the educators who worked there, have been either restructured or closed. Members of these two communities agreed to talk with me as part of a research project I conducted into the consequences communities face when the schools in those communities fail to meet standards of No Child Left Behind. The consequences of not meeting these standards proved life changing.

Parents in both of these communities spoke about a long history of children attending the community schools. They moved through the foundational elementary years, attended their adolescence in the middle schools, and finally graduated from the high schools. In the schooling process, everyone gained an identity with the schools that served to support a rich heritage throughout the community. Parents spoke of having pride in their schools, never thinking of them as not providing the opportunity for their children to gain the education they would need to move into adulthood and make career choices. In fact, the parents who grew up in these communities, and now had their children attending the same schools they attended, viewed the educational opportunities the same as their parents. The schools presented the opportunity for a better life. It was up to the children to reach out and make the most of their opportunity, and it was up to the parents to encourage, support, and provide the necessary guidance to help that opportunity become reality.

In years past the school district administration oversaw the leadership of the individual schools and provided the curriculum appropriate and suitable for the children attending the schools. Any problems with the faculty and staff were addressed through the administration of the school and school district. If the leadership provided and maintained the right environment for students to receive their education, the result was that the school flourished and had an excellent reputation.

In 2002, the No Child Left Behind Act was passed, forever changing the landscape of public education. Though many politicians have decried the act and made overtures to either update or radically change No Child Left Behind, it has remained intact. There are those who say that No Child Left Behind (NCLB) made needed improvements in public education; others who have been victims of the mandates of NCLB have a different story to tell. Many business leaders extol NCLB for forcing schools to adhere to standards that raise the bar for students and prepare them for college or careers. Others will say that high school students today are not graduating with the needed background and foundation necessary for college entrance or a promising career. This has resulted in remediation being a large part of incoming freshmen's curriculum.

Teachers today will most likely talk of an endless pattern of preparation to prepare students to take benchmark assessments that drill students on skill sets required to pass a standardized test. New teachers are overwhelmed at the degree of paperwork, data collection, and feedback required by administrators to ensure the proper performance of the students on the tests. Veteran teachers mourn the loss of any degree of autonomy within the walls of their classrooms. They feel trapped by scripted lessons that could just as easily be handled by a teaching assistant. One overwhelming constant is present in every public school in the country. This constant is the continual presence of preparation for the next test. The test is ever-present in all activities of the teachers, counselors, and administrators. This is the state of public education today. The current state of education is a result of thirty-plus years of education reform that have seen an increasing encroachment by the federal government into an area that, in the past, was reserved to the states. The passage of No Child Left Behind injected the federal government to such an extent that it fundamentally changed what takes place in the classroom and what is allowed to be taught by teachers of the core subjects.

This fundamental change came with the mandates NCLB dictated. The devastating effects of these mandates are addressed within the pages of this book. The information presented is an adaptation from research conducted in pursuit of a PhD in Educational Leadership by this researcher. The information contained within was collected from scholarly work, current writings in the field, and information obtained from educators entrenched in the day-to-day teaching environment created by NCLB mandates. Many of the resources used for documentation are current to within five years. Other sources go further back in time, however, as the current state of education has been decades in the making.

The current events unfolding today are the result of an incremental, well-planned agenda that has been fostered on an unaware public and an all-too-trusting education profession. Some of the narrative reflects my opinions. They are, however, opinions developed from years in the education profession and an abundance of research.

As a former middle school and high school principal, serving in the education profession as a teacher and administrator for thirty-four years, I have shaped my views on the state of education today using the lens of experience and time. I had the honor of serving as an administrator in public schools, both as an assistant principal and later as a principal, during each phase of the testing regimen in Texas (with the exception of the latest implementation, STAAR). It was not until I retired in 2007 and was removed from the demands and pressure of operating a public school that I was able to objectively evaluate my own educational paradigm. While I was working I experienced cognitive dissonance as it relates to my profession. I was convinced that through continued diligence, drive, and determination, a more educated student would emerge. It was my belief that the profession was on the right track and we were operating in the student's best interest.

The increased demands I felt to provide the proper leadership to get the desired results grew in intensity with each passing year. Virtually all curriculum decisions made were data-driven decisions required to have the best opportunity to obtain an accountability rating that met standards. All of this led to requiring faculty members to attend more and more staff development, identify those students with learning gaps as quickly as possible, and provide the necessary individual education plans that would hopefully correct any deficiencies. While all of this was productive in helping the student pass the state test, I was unaware of what the policy of No Child Left Behind was doing to the true educational opportunities for the students. In my eyes, student success and school success were linked to a label and a number on the accountability rating issued through the state and federal educational agencies. I was not aware that what was occurring was actually a limitation placed on information and knowledge—a limitation built around testing and preparation for the next testing cycle.

After retiring I continued to follow current events in education and became more keenly aware of some of the elements of No Child Left Behind that seemed problematic. The more I researched, the more it became evident that No Child Left Behind created an insurmountable task to meet the standards required. For many schools, especially in urban centers of poverty, the challenge to meet standards became next to impossible. This insurmountable task had nothing to do with teachers or administrators performing their daily jobs to the very best of their ability, but rather with the language used in No Child Left Behind mandates and the mechanism used to grade success or failure in meeting standards.

My concern for the current state of education grew when I looked at the broader picture of everything that was occurring in the country and the world at large. The federal government was showing a lack of priority for the education system. During this same time in 2010, the country was still suffering from the economic downturn that started in 2008. States were not getting the funds they were accustomed to receiving from the federal government. Due to funds not received from the federal government, the state education agency applied financial cuts to local school districts. At the local level, school districts were fighting for every dollar. For the first time in recent memory, teachers were laid off, resulting in a significant increase in classroom sizes. School districts were also affected through tax revenues being cut sharply due to the housing market collapse. The usual projections for revenue made by school districts failed to materialize, leaving district budgets in dire straits.

At this same time, President Obama started his education initiative called Race To The Top, where states had opportunities to compete for funds from the federal government. Some states, including Texas, opted not to take part in this competition because state officials saw strings attached to the federal money. As school districts struggled to operate with decreased funds, each school year the mandates required for meeting the standards of NCLB became more burdensome. Requirements in passing percentages rose without any regard for the difficulties the school districts were experiencing. The vise continued to tighten, and pressure mounted on administrators and teachers to ensure that students passed the test. As the stakes grew higher, with penalties for not meeting standards becoming unthinkable, teaching became more and more scripted to the test. While teachers were stretched to their limit straining to meet the demands of higher standards, teachers and administrators kept hearing reports of international comparisons indicating US children were getting a substandard education. Instead of being at the top of the rankings in reading, math, science, and social studies, the students in America's schools had dropped significantly from academic standings in the past. All of these issues were occurring as NCLB mandates were left in place, despite the cries from those in the profession denouncing the system as basically ineffective. The morale among teachers across the country reached record lows.

It became obvious that proper funding for education was not a priority. While the federal government restricted money to the states, foreign wars continued, and enormous bailouts to banks and corporations, which were seen as too big to fail, took place. It became quite clear that education was not seen as too big to fail. There was no bailout for school districts—only continued demands to meet the mandates of NCLB with less money and fewer teachers.

This led to soul-searching and in-depth reading on this researcher's part to determine why this paradox existed. Government officials, from both dominant parties, are extolling the need for better schools and educational opportunities, yet withholding the dollars needed to keep teachers' jobs and classroom sizes at workable numbers. If the NCLB mandates were to have a chance to succeed, at the very least, an adequate number of teachers were needed to cover the enrollment numbers.

By 2011 schools began to "fail" in greater numbers. The general public saw this as a result of poor teaching and dysfunctional administrative leadership. What the public did not understand was that the failure was a result of mandates built into NCLB law. The wording in one of the mandates of NCLB virtually guaranteed schools would eventually reach a point of failure due to not being able to keep up with the percentages required to meet standards.

Those in the education profession must realize what has occurred to our profession. Stating it bluntly, the education profession has been hijacked. This realization is needed before we can begin to reclaim what was once the best education system in the world. This researcher's interest lies in bringing information to light that will hopefully provide the needed knowledge for the education profession, and the general public, to understand this crisis in education and what the root cause for the crisis is. Equipped with proper knowledge and information, the educators who work so hard every day in the classroom and the parents who see the effects of high-stakes testing on their children, can begin to demand the changes necessary to reclaim the schools and take back the teaching profession.

The significance of the information contained in this book cannot be overemphasized. The events portrayed in this study are current and extremely important to the existing body of knowledge that has, to date, been written on the negative effects of No Child Left Behind (NCLB). Parents and their children, along with their communities, have been impacted greatly by the mandates of NCLB. The public is asking important questions that need addressing. Government officials are not providing the necessary answers, and the task of addressing the true needs is now left up to those in the education profession and the people in the communities that are affected.

A significant goal of this book is to bring clarity of the deception that has been perpetrated on the American people, and especially the education profession, as to the true nature and intent of NCLB. Why have the laws of No Child Left Behind been written in a manner that drives schools to failure? Why have the sanctions against schools been so punitive that it has forced teachers to teach a scripted lesson addressing only those essential elements that a student will see on the state test? Why has so much information that was previously taught by teachers been removed from curricula? Only information and knowledge seen on the test is that which is measured. Only that which is measured is valued. If it is not on the test, it is not valued, so therefore it is not taught. Why is there seemingly an agenda for the control of information and knowledge? It is time to set the record straight and get to the heart of why the education profession is in this current condition.

Those who agreed to participate in the research connected with this book bear witness to the impact NCLB mandates have on school communities. A look at the present state of education demonstrates this impact. There are three themes that run throughout the book. This book will explore how the present state of education developed. It will reveal the devastating damage perpetrated on the education establishment, parents, and children who are in schools struggling to meet standards of No Child Left Behind. Finally, the information contained in this book will expose the agenda for the control of information and knowledge.

CHAPTER 1

The Current State of Public
Education in America

Is the education system in America on the right track, or is it horribly flawed? That could be the fundamental question that needs answering. Our school officials at the state and federal level tell us we are on the right track. They tell us the achievement gap is narrowing and our children are receiving the education they need to compete in today's global market. In 2011 a funny thing happened, however, on the way to school reform. Schools all across America began to fail in record numbers. Washington called this a crisis in education. How apropos that the very entity that created the crisis was now decrying the crisis. Blue-ribbon panels were assembled to investigate this crisis of failure. An answer was needed to the ever-increasing number of schools that were not meeting standards. Washington's mantra was that if the standards were not met, something had to be done to rectify the situation. Experts from academia, corporations, independent businessmen and women, politics, and even the entertainment industry gathered in some of these made-for-TV investigative reports to deliver their magic pill that was going to take a kid from urban America and make him or her excited about attending school. What they should have said was, make him or her excited about wanting to take, and do well on, a standardized test. The experts talked about creating a spark in a child that would make learning fun. They talked about the joys of reading and the exhilaration of logically putting your thoughts down on paper. They discussed the disparity between urban minority children when compared to their suburban counterparts, called the *achievement gap*. Never once, however, did any expert who had numerous credentials by his or her name, mention the real reason why the schools were failing.

Schools fail because they fail to meet standards. This is how it is worded in the accountability system of the state and federal education agencies. Schools either *meet standards* or they *fail to meet standards*. These standards refer to the *percentage* of students passing in their *like group* on the standardized test given to students once a year. The like groups will be explained shortly, but suffice it to say that all students are placed into groups based on ethnicity, gender, language ability, or learning disability that qualify for special education services. It has nothing to do with the number of students who learn their course requirements and pass their classes. It has nothing to do with the dedication and hard work of the teachers, counselors, and administrators who are doing everything in their power to get their students to be successful. It has *everything* to do with the percentages of students who pass the test within their categorized group. The percentage required in the groups rises with each successive year. When the percentages become unreachable, the school fails.

Due to the manner in which the debate over school failure is framed, the public's viewpoint is that teachers aren't working hard enough or smart enough, and principals aren't showing proper leadership. This lack of effort and leadership is also the perception presented by the media and government officials. This perception of by the public, media and government officials, however, is not what fails a school. People from business who understand standards as a means of measuring productivity are in full agreement that schools should have standards. There needs to be criteria that define what a child needs to learn and when he or she needs to learn it. There is no argument with that point. This is what is termed a scope and sequence, and teachers have always followed a scope and sequence with their curricula. What the general public does not understand is that these curriculum-essential elements of learning are not the standards that determine if a school fails. It is the percentage of passing in the groups that are evaluated for accountability that determines pass or fail for the school and the school district. The groups where students are placed are called by different names in different school districts throughout the country. The groups are called either subgroups or sub-populations. For the sake of clarity

I will use the term subgroups. Each subgroup stands alone when it comes to accountability and *meeting the standards* or *failing to meet the standards*.

In Texas, where I have spent my career, the accountability system of the Texas Education Agency divides a school's report card, for measuring the state test results, into subgroups. This occurred in 1991. At the same time, a more rigorous state test was developed. This latest evolution of the state standardized test was called TAAS, or Texas Assessment of Academic Skills. Every state had a similar test that was governed through its state education agency. The students were divided into subgroups and were categorized into five groups: All Students, African American, Hispanic, White, and Economically Disadvantaged. At this time the federal government was not involved in the accountability system. School districts were doing reasonably well under this testing format. Lessons had not become scripted yet, and teachers were not teaching to the test. There was still a level of flexibility for teachers to inject their own expertise and experience into their lessons.

This changed in 2002 with the advent of No Child Left Behind under the George W. Bush administration. For the first time the federal government was now dictating to the states a measure of accountability that would forevermore bring the schools under federal jurisdiction. The *mechanism of control* brought in with No Child Left Behind was called Adequate Yearly Progress (AYP). Along with this new mechanism of control, the U.S. Department of Education added two more subgroups. These subgroups were Special Education and Limited English Proficient (LEP).

Very important to understand is this basic point: the intent of subgroups was to force school officials to address groups of students that were not performing well on the standardized test. There was a gap in the passing percentage in some of the groups. Because this *achievement gap*, which still exists, had more to do with poverty than it did ethnicity, the very students that NCLB purports to help are the very students that are hurt the most. This will be discussed further in the text, but suffice it to say now that the reason for this is that No Child Left Behind does not address social conditions that affect children of poverty.

Table 1 helps to illustrate the subgroups according to state and federal guidelines. Of interest is the caveat that the federal government put on special education, which the state had left alone. The federal guidelines placed a 3% cap on special education students that can be screened out of taking the normal standardized test that regular education students are assigned to take. That means the only special education students that can exempt out of taking the test are developmentally challenged students and severely handicapped students. This criterion did away with resource, or basic, classes. It placed all special education students not included in the 3% in with the regular education population. While the general public may see this measure as inconsequential, for teachers across America it posed a dilemma. With more students in the general education classrooms, more time is required from the teacher to address the special needs of the students in the class with unique disabilities. The teacher is held accountable for the outcomes of all students in his or her class, so the extra time allocated for ensuring all students are prepared for the test takes on new importance.

Table 1

Comparison of State and Federal Accountability

State Accountability 5 subgroups (All students, African American, Hispanic, White, Economically Disadvantaged)	Federal Accountability (AYP) 7 subgroups (Texas 5, Limited English Proficient, Special Education)
5 subjects (Reading/ELA, Mathematics, Writing, Social Studies, Science)	2 Subjects (Reading/ELA, Mathematics)
Grades 3–11	Grades 3–8 & 10
Standards – Reading/ELA, Writing, Social Studies 70%; Mathematics 65%; Science 60%	Standards – Reading/ELA 80%; Mathematics 75%
No caps on special education alternative assessments.	3% cap on special education alternative assessments.

Note: From "Understanding Texas Public School Accountability," News Release Klein ISD, August, 15, 2011.

With a clear understanding of subgroups, the mechanism that moved schools to failure is easier to comprehend. The AYP system is the mechanism that drove schools to failure. Think back to 2002 when President Bush declared that by 2014 all students would be proficient on the test. This received wide acclaim and was accepted by most everyone as a wonderful goal to strive to accomplish. The problem, though, is that President Bush did not exclaim it as a worthy goal. He wrote it into law. In order to reach 100% proficiency, schools had to begin moving upward in their percentages applied to the student groups used for accountability. This means the subgroups, each subgroup graded independently, had to reach the percentage of passage established for that year. As the years went by from 2002 onward, the percentages went up, and so did the percentage of schools that failed. This is the AYP mechanism of control that brought schools to failure. A particular student population that did not receive proper instruction from their teachers did not bring on failure. It was the mechanism of control, the AYP accountability system, which incrementally over a period of time brought schools to failure. More importantly to comprehend, it did so by intent. This deliberate intent will be demonstrated throughout this book.

The accountability system installed with No Child Left Behind is an educational accountability program that hurts the very students that it advertised to help. It did more to widen the achievement gap than close it. It was designed to bring schools to failure so panic would break out across the educational landscape and acceptance would be given to a new brand of education that finally delivered total federal control over the states' jurisdiction of public education. The next chapter will deal more with the federal education system that created the problem with the schools throughout the country and how failing to meet standards placed schools on the road to restructure and closure.

CHAPTER 2

Facing the Reality of No Child Left Behind

In the fall of 2012 I began to research an area of Austin, Texas, that was experiencing restructuring in the schools located on the east side of the city. This small but culturally vibrant community on the east side of Austin was in the process of losing one of the most important identifiers that brought them all together as a community of people—their neighborhood schools. These schools supported several generations of community members as they received their primary, middle, and high school education. When I looked into the phenomenon that was occurring in east Austin, I found out the elementary school (Whittaker, 2012), where generations of children received their primary education, was now renamed and restructured. It was operating as a public charter school. The middle school was being monitored and slated for takeover by the charter management company hired by Austin Independent School District (ISD). The high school in the feeder path of the elementary and middle school was scheduled to follow in the same restructuring path if the superintendent and board of trustees follow the same course of action. Before you cast too much blame on the school district, it is important to keep in mind that the course of action required of the district was mandated through NCLB law. It was federal law that dictated Adequate Yearly Progress (AYP) Standards that caused the schools to fail and therefore not meet standards. District officials had no choice but to follow the law.

My research took me to another community, located just north of Houston, Texas, where an entire school district was dissolved. The Commissioner of Education for the State of Texas, acting through the Texas Education Agency, closed the North Forest Independent School District and disbanded the board of trustees due to years of failure to meet AYP federal standards and unacceptable ratings from the State of Texas. The school district was merged into the very large Houston Independent School District located next door just to the south of North Forest ISD. Upon closure of the school district, every professional employee lost his or her job. What happened in the east-side community in Austin and the North Forest ISD is a microcosm of what happened in communities across the country. To understand what they went through as a school and community is to understand the endgame of No Child Left Behind.

With the reauthorization of the Elementary and Secondary Education Act of 1965, termed No Child Left Behind (NCLB) in 2002, along with its accountability system, schools are moving in a progressive path that ultimately leads to school failure and restructure (Mead, 2007) if the schools are not able to improve their accountability ratings. Provisions in NCLB address schools that fail to achieve prescribed mandates for Adequate Yearly Progress (AYP). Across the country schools have reached the point of AYP failure and are now in the process of restructuring, which is mandated through NCLB law (Texas Education Agency, 2012b) and carried out by the state education agency. The parents of the east-side community of Austin and the educational professionals and parents of the North Forest ISD give testimony in this book of their struggle with the mandates of NCLB when taken to their final stage of school reform.

The Issue of Evaluation and Accountability

A closer look at some historical events will bring clarity and understanding to how the situation in Austin and North Forest ISD developed. In the fall of 2012, Chicago teachers were engulfed in a union strike that had them taking part in a walkout. Thousands of children were out of school over issues that the teachers' union was negotiating with Chicago's city officials. At stake were the usual pay discrepancies, but also at issue was the new evaluation policy that tied job security to the outcomes of the students' state assessment. To state it differently, the teachers' evaluations were linked to how their students performed on the state-mandated assessment, which was a hallmark of No Child Left Behind. Looming just ahead was the 2014 mandate of 100% proficiency on the math and reading portions of the mandated state assessment that was written into No Child Left Behind policy:

> Chicago Teachers Union President Karen Lewis is critical of Mayor Rahm Emanuel's push to make great use of standardized tests in teacher reviews, calling the process flawed. Union officials say the system wouldn't do enough to take into account outside factors such as poverty, crime and homelessness. (Omer, 2012, para. 3)

The evaluation of the students' overall performances on the mandated assessment lay at the heart of the issue. The variables that came into play with individual students substantially differed on any given day and had a bearing on the students' performance. The difference in economic and social conditions in various regions of the country made the one-size-fits-all approach problematic. In a previous study on school accountability, Popham (1999) highlighted the problems with judging school quality and effectiveness by how students performed on a standardized achievement test. "Because student performances on standardized achievement tests are heavily influenced by three causative factors, only one of which is linked to instructional quality, asserting that low or high test scores are caused by the quality of instruction is illogical" (Popham, 1999, para. 33). According to Popham, the three causative factors are "(1) what's taught in school, (2) a student's native intellectual ability, and (3) a student's out-of-school learning" (1999, para. 36). Yet written into law by President George W. Bush is the mandate that by 2014 all students must show proficiency on both the reading and math portion of the state assessment. In order to get districts prepared for the 2014 date, the proficiency percentage continues to steadily climb each year. In 2011, the AYP percentages required to meet standards were (Texas Education Agency, 2011) 80% in Reading/Language Arts and 75% in Math. In the 2012–2013 school year, the percentages climb higher; and by the testing dates of 2014, the 100%

mandate is required. Superintendents all over the nation know that means failure for their schools and their district.

In order to allow school districts to escape the 100% mandate, President Obama reached out to the states and agreed to extend a waiver option that included in the waiver package an exemption of the 100% mandate. If the states could come up with an acceptable alternative plan (Center on Education Policy, 2012) that conformed to the provisions laid down in the waiver package, then the state was excluded from the 2014 mandate. The plan submitted by each state had to contain an increase in professional development and a new acceptable evaluation for teachers and principals that were tied into accountability standards related back to the state assessment. The idea of starting over with a new evaluation system is already proving extremely costly to the states seeking to be in compliance just to submit an application for the waiver.

> California would need to spend up to $3.1 billion to implement teacher evaluations, adopt new learning standards, purchase new textbooks and other costs before the state can qualify for a waiver from the much-criticized No Child Left Behind testing rules, according to a state report. (Leal, 2011, para. 1)

Another provision for gaining the waiver is the states agree to follow a new set of standards for teachers and their instruction (Leal, 2011). These standards are consistent from state to state for all who accept the waiver. As of late 2013, 45 states were approved for waivers, with five states still in review (U.S. Department of Education, n.d. b).

Whether or not it was a good idea for the Obama administration to even offer a waiver is a matter of debate in education and legal circles. President Obama called his waiver plan the ESEA Flexibility Plan. According to the American Enterprise Institute, "Indeed, the central thesis of this piece is that the administration's ESEA Flexibility plan carries three serious risks— primarily legal, but political and operational as well—that may prove to be its undoing" (Riley, 2012, para. 8). Two key issues leave much to consider with the waiver plan. First, is it legal (Riley, 2012)? Can President Obama legislate from the executive branch? The second issue is the waiver plan leaves two education systems operational at the same time—those under the waiver and those under NCLB. All of this transpired while schools and teachers under NCLB were left to live under the penalties of the policy.

In order for states to qualify for the waiver option, President Obama (Resmovits, 2012) created some conditions that must be adhered to by the states for acceptance into the waiver program. States were to build college-and-career-readiness standards and increased professional development into their education plans, and they were to link teacher evaluations to the results of their students' outcomes on the state assessment. A critical component was the college-and-career-readiness standards that were equated with the Common Core State Standards (Riley, 2012). Very important to also include in the state's plan to receive the waiver, is every state that qualified to receive a waiver had to demonstrate its plan to move students to 100% proficiency. The carrot extended by the waiver only delayed the AYP mandate for 100% proficiency; it did not remove the mandate. This is explained in more detail later.

The School Improvement Program

Of interest in understanding how AYP moves schools and school districts to failure is to explore the School Improvement Program. Schools and school districts that are under Title I are mandated to enter the School Improvement Program once they fail to meet standards in the same subgroup two years in a row. If the school or school district stay in the School Improvement Program for five years in a row the state must move in and take drastic action. Five options (U.S. Department of Education, n.d. a) are available to a district when one of its Title I schools has five consecutive years of AYP failure in the same category (subgroup); the options are as follow:

1. Reopen the school as a public charter school.
2. Replace all or most of school staff, including the principal.
3. Enter into a contract with an entity, such as a private management company, with a demonstrated record of effectiveness to operate the school.
4. Have the state take over the school.

5. Impose another major restructuring of the school's governance arrangement (Texas Education Agency, 2012 b).

Depending on the communities where these failing schools were located, when the failed school was restructured, a large percentage of school districts chose option five since that option offered the least disruption to the school. A report from the Center on Education Policy entitled *A Call to Restructure Restructuring* (Scott, 2008) indicated that while most were selecting option five, some school districts were taking the charter school, option one. In the Austin school district, researched in this study, the option chosen was option three, which was to engage a private management company hired to work with the school district to improve the neighborhood schools in question in the east-side community.

In public charter schools, whether they are a Charter Management Organization (CMO) or an Education Management Organization (EMO), students must take the state standardized test (Texas Education Agency, 2013a) that public school students take each year. This fact puts charter schools (which are funded partially through taxpayer dollars) in the same predicament that public schools face. In order to conform to AYP standards, the teachers are required to spend more time on essential elements found on the test in order to comply with the yearly AYP standards. This holds true for public school instruction as well.

In order to increase teacher accountability, any state approved to receive the waiver must have the teacher appraisal system linked (McNeil, 2013) to the outcomes of the students on the state test. This policy came under intense scrutiny (McNeil) by state education agencies and teacher unions. The U.S. Department of Education held firm on this requirement and by 2013 had only approved (McNeil) 12 states' evaluation systems of the 45 states currently under the waiver provisions. With the teacher evaluation linked to the testing outcomes, the likelihood of more scripted lesson plans (Ravitch, 2010) is virtually assured. "Evaluating teachers in relation to student test scores will have many adverse consequences. It will make the current standardized tests of basic skills more important than ever, and even more time and resources will be devoted to raising scores on these tests" (2010, para. 4).

Because technology has become such a huge part of the instructional day for students in today's schools, there is a paradox in the instruction that purports to enhance the knowledge base of the student, while at the same time limiting their learning choices through the technology. On one hand, both NCLB and the TEKS expect teachers to infuse technology in ways that guide, empower, and prepare students for our exponentially growing technological world. On the other hand, they limit assessment of student knowledge and acquisition of these skills to a standardized test that reduces solutions to choices A, B, C, or D. (Brown, n.d., para. 11)

Dr. Diane Ravitch, a senior policy advisor in the Department of Education under the Clinton administration, defines this shift in instructional approach very aptly in her quoting of Campbell's law from the work of Daniel Koretz, a psychometrician at Harvard University. "Koretz contends that coaching students for state tests produces test score inflation and the illusion of progress" (Ravitch, 2010, p.159). Campbell's law states:

The more any quantitative social indicator is used for social decision-making, the more subject it will be to corruption pressures and the more apt it will be to distort and corrupt the social processes it is intended to monitor. (p. 160)

Ravitch demonstrates the lack of reliability in this instructional approach when she references Koretz's work and his thoughts on changing the dynamic of the instruction to meet a testing outcome. "The changes induced by accountability pressures corrupt the very purpose of schooling by causing practitioners to focus on the measure rather than on the goals of education" (p. 160).

Standardized Testing for Accountability

With the advent of the computer, humanity is on a continual journey of expanded knowledge and readily available information. Since the early 1990s, the computer played an increasing role in the teaching of students in public schools across America. At the same time as computer usage was on the rise, a common standardized test saw increased use as the determination of student overall success. In 1982 Texas mandated its first statewide assessment for all school children. All students would take the same assessment, or test, at the same time of the school year (Ott, 2010). The only students not taking the test were special education students that were exempted by committee. This standardized state assessment in Texas was called the Texas Assessment of Basic Skills (TABS). The test was used primarily for diagnostic purposes, was not required for graduation, and did not carry accountability measures for the schools. Similar tests were administered in other states. With each passing year, the relationship of school accountability to the success of the student on the mandated state assessment grew increasingly important. With increased accountability came an increased emphasis on the essential elements that the teachers were to include in their lessons in the core four subjects (Language Arts, Math, Science, and Social Studies).

The following progressions of tests that follow apply to Texas, but similar actions were occurring across the country. In 1984 (Ott, 2010) the difficulty and rigor of the test increased as the Texas Educational Assessment of Minimal Skills (TEAMS) came into Texas public schools. With the TEAMS, students were required to pass the test in order to receive their high school diploma. This was a test that addressed minimal skills, not basic skills. In this case, the term *basic* denoted a lower requirement than *minimal*.

In the eyes of the state education agency, the state-mandated assessment grew to be the single determinant in evaluating whether a school was a success or a failure. "In 1991, the Texas Legislature believed students needed to achieve more than just minimum skills. So once again the ante was 'upped' and a new testing program came on the scene" (Ott, 2010, para. 1). This update of the test was called the Texas Assessment of Academic Skills (TAAS).

After TAAS the rigor was again increased when the Texas Assessment of Knowledge and Skills (TAKS) was initiated in 2003. Now the students of Texas have the latest evolution of the state test. This is called the State of Texas Assessment of Academic Readiness (STAAR). STAAR was first field-tested in the 2011–2012 school year, and in the 2012–2013 school year students began taking the test for accountability purposes.

With each update of the assessment came an increased measure for passing the test. What was once a measure of basic skills (Ott, 2010) grew into a test that became a challenge for many students in the public school system to pass. When the student's passage of the test became a requirement for graduation, as it did in Texas with the TAAS, the graduation rates of the schools were affected. This set in motion a cascading effect for teachers and district curriculum specialists. With the graduation requirement in effect, teachers were forced to examine their teaching strategies to aid students in passage of the test. It became a higher priority for teachers to conform their instruction to the elements that would be seen on the state test.

A New Way to Teach

Having all students taught under the same curriculum standards in order to achieve the required outcome on a standardized test would not be possible if it were not for a method of instruction called Outcomes-Based Education. Outcomes-Based Education (OBE) is a part of the toolbox used by educators for daily instruction. It has gone by other names, such as Mastery Learning, Back to Basics, Direct Instruction, and Performance-Based Education, but a more clear name for the instructional method is Outcomes-Based Education, since the measure of its validity comes in the outcomes or scores a student produces when evaluated. Two of the proponents of OBE, venerated throughout the years by aspiring teachers, are B. F. Skinner and Benjamin Bloom.

Skinner is best known for his Skinner Box, from which his experiments with stimulus-response brought his operant conditioning theory of social behavior. "Skinner's theory of operant conditioning was based on the work of Thorndike (1905). Edward Thorndike studied learning in animals using a puzzle box to propose the theory known as the *Law of Effect*" (McLeod, 2007, para. 5). Skinner took Thorndike's law of effect and added the term reinforcement. McLeod goes on to say about Skinner's reinforcement theory, "Behavior which is reinforced tends to be repeated (i.e. strengthened); behavior which is not reinforced tends to die out-or be extinguished (i.e. weakened)" (2007, para. 6).

The shaping of a person's behavior through reinforcement, or the lack of reinforcement, is now fundamental for behaviorists. The concept of reinforcement as a teaching strategy is drilled into every prospective teacher by colleges of education throughout the country. It is also an item all evaluators look for when assessing a teacher's performance in the classroom. B. F. Skinner is best known for his 1971 best seller *Beyond Freedom and Dignity*. In this very influential book, Skinner spoke of society and how it could be shaped to avoid the pitfalls that have plagued mankind for eons.

A most interesting theory that Skinner puts forth in the book is the idea that, based upon his earlier research into animal motivation and control, humans are essentially animals that could be controlled by using his previously discovered and published observations about the domination of animals through motivation and deprivation. Humans are subject to the same laws of stimulus-response that he observed in his rat boxes, or what have come to be known as Skinner boxes in psychological circles (Raver, 2006, para. 2).

The work of Benjamin Bloom is equally important to the development of proper methods that were established for teacher education. Bloom's taxonomy of learning objectives and his subsequent differentiation of the objectives into the affective, cognitive, and psychomotor domains formed the most fundamental elements of how children learn and became widely accepted throughout colleges of education. Bloom's theories were incorporated into his Mastery Learning, which became commonplace in teacher education programs from the 1970s onward. For the purpose of this study, the link between Mastery Learning and OBE is important. It is worth noting that some education historians see little separation between Mastery Learning, Direct Instruction, and Outcomes-Based Education.

> Professor Benjamin Bloom, called the Father of Outcome Based Education, summarized it well: 'The purpose of education and the schools is to change the thoughts,

feelings and actions of students. … A large part of what we call 'good teaching' is the teacher's ability to attain affective objectives through challenging the students' fixed beliefs and getting them to discuss issues.' (Kjos, n.d.)

Of note in the above quote is not only Berit Kjos's view that Bloom is linked with OBE, but also a glimpse is given into Bloom's beliefs about the affective domain of the child learner and the teacher's ability to effect change with fixed belief systems. Charlotte Iserbyt, Senior Policy Advisor in the Department of Education in President Reagan's first administration, sees the link with Bloom and OBE and Mastery Learning.

> Mastery learning uses Skinnerian methodology (operant conditioning) in order to obtain 'predictable' results. Benjamin Bloom, the father of Mastery Learning, says that 'the purpose of education is to change the thoughts, actions and feelings of students.' Mastery Learning (ML), and its fraternal twin Direct Instruction (DI) are key components of Outcome-Based Education (OBE) and Effective School Research (ESR). (Iserbyt, 1999, p. 4)

Iserbyt, considered an excellent educational historian, also gives the same quote that Kjos reported on Bloom's thoughts on the purpose of education. She also makes the connection between all three learning theories: Mastery Learning, Direct Instruction, and Outcomes-Based Education. The point of the discussion of Skinner and Bloom is mainly to point out that both men are revered in colleges of teacher education throughout the country and that both men frame their theories of learning around the outcomes produced by the students in conjunction with behavior modification.

Direct Instruction (Whittaker, 2012) is the method used by the public charter school company working in conjunction with the Austin ISD presented in this study. Instead of a traditional instructional method that focused on teacher inputs to the student, the Charter Management Organization (CMO) adopted a computer-dependent "direct instruction model" (para. 5) that focused on student outcomes. A closer look into OBE shows more of the intent of its use in today's classroom and the gradual incremental infusion of OBE across the nation's state education systems. Manno (1994) published a comprehensive investigative report into OBE's beginnings and its proponents' push to make OBE the preferred method of instruction to lead schools into the age of accountability. Manno gave insight to what distinguishes OBE from traditional instructional models and its use in the classroom to measure predetermined learning objectives.

> There has been a fundamental shift in the last third of this century – which is not to say in all quarters—when it comes to effectively evaluating educational quality. Previously, the conventional wisdom judged quality in terms of inputs: intentions and efforts, institutions and services, resources and spending. In more recent years, however, focus has increased on outputs: products and results, outcomes and effects – with an emphasis on core academic subjects ... What are our children learning, and how well are they learning it? (Manno, 1994, para. 12)

The watershed event (Manno, 1994) that changed the paradigm of educational approach throughout the nation originated in the 1983 report *A Nation at Risk,* commissioned by T.H. Bell, Secretary of Education. In this report from the U.S. Department of Education, the educational system, that was the established order, was seen as deficient, and a new approach was seen as mandatory if the nation were to compete on the world stage.

> The report's basic criticism was that America's young people were not learning enough, and it made clear that the input focus and resource-based strategies of the mid-1960s and the Great Society had failed to improve the nation's education results significantly. Weak academic achievement, therefore, was the key education problem. (Manno, 1994, para. 38)

Outcomes-Based Education grew into the preferred method of instruction, which synced perfectly with the use of standardized tests to measure the outcomes of what students had learned and how the school performed its job. A closer look at OBE as the preferred instructional method for NCLB is critical to understand in relation to the background of the issues in this study.

If Outcomes-Based Education were producing better schools through quality programs that produced well-educated children ready to take on the world in global competition, the proof would be in the outcomes. The rise of school failures in their inability to consistently achieve Adequate Yearly Progress standards through the policies of NCLB indicated that the method of instruction used to prepare students for taking a state-mandated assessment was flawed. If the entire NCLB policy and requirements were successful, schools would be moving closer to the mandated AYP percentages with each passing year. The method of evaluation of the public school's effectiveness and the method of instruction used for educating the students through increased use of standardized tests over the past 30 years has not produced the type of results that would warrant praise for the program and continuation of its mandates. The low graduation rates (Dillon, 2009) in urban schools when compared with those of suburban schools is clear evidence that NCLB is not living up to its proclaimed prestige as the system that would put America's children as the leader in global comparisons.

A closer look at the accountability system used to grade schools and school districts on the testing outcomes, and the tight controls it places on instruction, is needed if we are to find a source to blame for the low graduation rates and poor testing performance. According to Secretary of Education Arne Duncan (McNeil, 2011), under No Child Left Behind's punitive Adequate Yearly Progress (AYP) standards, 82% of America's public schools failed in 2010. If the Secretary of Education is denouncing the current policies and not taking the steps to radically change the policies, should we not be alarmed? By leaving the accountability system intact, the system will not change no matter which curriculum is used to teach students. As the statistics show, by 2012 most of America's schools were failing—more with each passing year. With the standards for a school to pass and be considered successful being higher for 2013—92% passing percentage in Math and 93% in Reading/ELA—the percentage of failing schools will only climb higher.

Only That Which is Measured is Valued

The education a student receives at the hands of public education has changed over the last 30 years. From the traditional style of teacher-led instruction, based on the transfer of knowledge from the teacher to the student via a variety of instructional methods, education in public schools, as discussed previously, has moved to an Outcomes-Based Education system, where knowledge learned is predetermined and measured through a state assessment. Due to the high stakes involved with the accountability system, teachers began to place increased value on the essential elements that the state test measures. That which is measured becomes that which is valued. Some questions arise with an understanding of value in instruction. How has this change in education in America affected the quality of education a student in today's education system receives? What is the impact on teacher morale? If information and knowledge are predetermined and controlled, who is the controller? Where is the education system headed in the future, and what role will the parent play in his or her child's education? This study centered on these questions and investigated the phenomenon of school restructuring due to the failure of the public schools to meet federally mandated AYP percentages and state-mandated accountability standards. This study also investigated how accountability and AYP standards potentially tie back to the limitations placed on the acquisition of knowledge and the control of information.

The Reality of School Restructuring

When Austin began the restructuring program, it garnered attention across the country. In the community affected by the new policies, it rallied the parents to action. A community action organization was established called Pride of the Eastside, the purpose of which was to engage the school district and force it to pay attention to the citizens' wants and desires. There was a fear in the east-side community that the school district was moving ahead with its plans without listening to what parents and students were saying about the realities taking place in the schools and the community. This fear was realized when the school district announced in the spring of 2012 that the elementary school would be turned into a charter school for the next school year, with management of the school coming from outside the district. The community had voiced a strong desire that a charter management company not be hired. When the district chose not to listen to this request, it forced the community and the parents to take action.

As mentioned, the activity in Austin gained the national spotlight and was addressed at a statewide meeting of school superintendents and other state education officials. On the same day, another meeting was held in the Eastside Memorial High School gymnasium, organized by Pride of the Eastside. In the gym of Eastside Memorial, people from the neighborhoods gathered to hear a prominent individual from academia who had entered into the education reform debate. Dr. Diane Ravitch, addressed the issues and openly discussed the process that led to Austin ISD moving forward with their plan to begin the restructuring of the eastside schools. At issue was the high school's inability to make the AYP federal standards for five years in a row.

Dr. Ravitch, a former U.S. Assistant Secretary of Education under the Clinton administration and currently a research professor at New York University, spoke to two different audiences in her trip to Texas. The date was Sunday, September 30, 2012, and Dr. Ravitch spoke to the gathering of superintendents from across the state on the condition of the education system in the country. Dr. Ravitch addressed the Texas school superintendents in the morning, and then later in the day, she arrived at Eastside Memorial High School. This was ground zero in the fight to save neighborhood schools in Texas. Parents, teachers, concerned community members, and education activists—who worked to save public education, get rid of NCLB, and bring back a measure of sanity for the children and their education—were in the audience. Dr. Ravitch understands the testing industry and has written extensively on the topic. She was involved in reading and proofing many of the standardized tests that were used in the early years of the reform movement. Dr. Ravitch explained that many of the tests were filled with errors. There were errors in measurement (Ravitch, 2010) and design, and some were just factually incorrect. She offered some insight in how the education community and the general public had been manipulated over the years about the achievement gap.

The notion that minority children were way behind their White counterparts was not based on reliable data (Ravitch, 2010). The fact is that minority children today are far beyond the students of fifty years ago. Yet the achievement gap between African Americans and Hispanics when compared to their White counterparts remains significant. The answer to this dilemma is more likely found in demographics than in test accountability standards.

> Poor children can learn and excel, but the odds are against them. Reformers like to say that 'demographics is not destiny,' but saying so doesn't make it true: demography is powerful. Every testing program shows a tight correlation between family income and test scores, whether it is the SAT, the ACT, the federal testing program, or state tests. (Ravitch, 2011, para. 21)

The greatest improvement in closing the achievement gap came in the 1970s and early '80s. This is when most of the desegregation (Ravitch, 2011) finally began to show improvements and many of the poverty issues were finally beginning to be turned around. The gains were not because of testing (Ravitch, 2011); they were about improving poverty and giving all children equal access to quality education.

At the close of the meeting in the high school gym, the crowd began their exit, and many of those in the audience extended thanks to Dr. Ravitch for caring enough to come to their community. This researcher was in attendance and could feel the appreciation for Dr. Ravitch but also could feel a sense of uncertainty. There was no resolution at the meeting, only concern for what may lie ahead for the community, the parents, and their children. The fact remains that NCLB, with all of its mandates, is public school law and must be followed.

Follow the Money

Attention is now turned to the business entities that stand to gain financially from public school failure. This reform movement, sometimes called school choice, can really be seen for its true direction when one understands the people behind the movement and the dollars that control their actions. Philanthropist Eli Broad established the Broad Foundation. Broad and his wife, Edythe, have assets of 2.1 billion dollars (Broad

Foundation, 2012), and they are putting their money into the foundation to create a better education for low-performing schools in predominately urban settings. During the last 30 years, education has become big business.

> The American educational system today is a $500–600 billion enterprise, funded overwhelmingly by public dollars, with billions of dollars in services and products being outsourced, and with political lobbying groups like the Democrats for Education Reform, financed by hedge-fund millionaires, leading the push to further outsource. The public educational system has always had ties to the business sector, including business leaders themselves and the philanthropies funded by business fortunes. But that influence has not always looked the same. Despite the fact that philanthropic giving has never constituted more than 1 percent of total educational funding, in recent years a handful of millionaires and billionaires have come to exert influence over educational policy and practice like at no other time in American history. (Kumashiro, 2012, para. 3)

School failure and the subsequent restructuring of the schools are seen as opportunities for corporations and foundations to make huge profits.

> The two leading venture philanthropies, the Gates Foundation and the Broad Foundation, do include among their grantees historically liberal organizations like the teacher unions. However, their funding priorities and strategic initiatives are so framed by neoliberalism, and their partnerships with conservative organizations and leaders so extensive, that their impact is indistinguishable from that of the conservative foundations. (2012, para. 23)

Who is the recipient of all this money? Most of the money is directed (Kumashiro, 2012) into public charter schools, technology, and computer software.

Examples of Public Charter Schools

Foundation- and taxpayer-funded charter schools are divided into two groups. The two primary groups are Charter Management Organizations (CMOs) and Education Management Organizations (EMOs). Both CMOs and EMOs are private companies that function to assist an existing charter school in its operations and management tasks or with a local school district to assist with low-performing public schools. CMOs are nonprofit charter school companies, and EMOs are for-profit corporations.

School districts have the ability to contract with a CMO or EMO (Texas Education Agency, 2013a) to assist them with their Title I schools that are due for restructuring under NCLB guidelines and mandates. The Local Education Agency (LEA) can apply for a grant through the U.S. Department of Education and the State Education Agency (SEA), called a School Improvement Grant, to get the necessary funds to contract with an EMO or a CMO. The funds are made available through provisions in Title I.

> School Improvement Grants, authorized under Section 1003(g) of Title I of the Elementary and Secondary Education Act of 1965 (Title I or ESEA), are grants, through State Educational Agencies (SEAs), to Local Educational Agencies (LEAs) for use in Title I schools identified for improvement, corrective action, or restructuring that demonstrate the greatest need for the funds and the strongest commitment to use the funds to provide adequate resources in order to raise substantially the achievement of their students so as to enable the schools to make adequate yearly progress and exit improvement status. (Texas Education Agency, 2013b, para. 1)

Examples of CMOs are KIPP Academies, Rocketship Charter Schools, Green Dot Charter Schools, and Yes Preparatory. CMOs are independent charters and operate inside a public school district. In some cases, like that of KIPP Academies and Yes Prep in Houston, Texas (Mellon, 2013), the charter school is actually located within an existing public school. This is now done in the Spring Branch Independent School District, located just west of Houston. KIPP Academy and Yes Prep have partnered with the school district's Landrum Middle School and Northbrook Middle School to have a charter school within the same building. "But Spring Branch is one of a few school systems nationwide that has embraced its high-performing rivals, allowing KIPP and YES this year to start their own campuses within two of the district's middle schools" (Mellon, 2013, para. 3). A foundation has come forward to help in the effort.

> The big question, of course, is whether this budding partnership will result in students acquiring a better education. The Bill and Melinda Gates Foundation believes so strongly in the cooperation that it made a $2.1 million donation to the Spring Branch partnership. It is donating a total of $25 million to seven districts nationwide. (Texas Education Agency, 2013b, para. 6)

Education Management Organizations, or EMOs, are different. Not only are they for-profit companies, but they also work with school districts to manage the schools in the district that have reached the failure point.

> EMOs contract with school districts and charter-granting bodies to use tax money and venture capital to operate public schools. EMOs range in size from the largest, Edison Schools, which operates more than 130 schools, to firms that operate single (largely charter) schools. Other relatively large EMOs that focus exclusively on public school operation include Mosaica Education, National Heritage Academies, Chancellor Beacon Academies, and Aspire Public Schools. Some EMOs, such as Nobel Learning Communities, own and operate private schools as well. (Hentschke, Oschman, & Snell, 2003, para. 3)

Accountability and AYP

The driving forces that allow EMOs and CMOs to have lucrative businesses due to school failure and their need for improvement is now addressed. The engine that drives these companies to rush and get the contracts once the schools fail comes from two different systems, both tied to No Child Left Behind. One source is the state accountability system, which grades schools on how well the school performed overall on the state-mandated assessment. The states are in charge of grading the individual schools and their school districts. Each year schools get their label based on the results from the previous year's tests. In Texas during the TAKS years, 2001-2012, schools were labeled exemplary, recognized, acceptable, or unacceptable. This labeling changed with the implementation of the new STAAR test in 2013. At this point, the state adopted the other accountability labeling system, that of the federal government that used Adequate Yearly Progress (AYP) to grade the nation's schools. There are only two categories of AYP: *met standards* or *failed to meet standards*.

Referring back to Table 1 in chapter 1, the federal and state accountability systems are compared. The table reflects the percentage of proficiency on the state assessment required for the 2010–2011 school year and also delineates the subgroups that are required to meet the same proficiency percentages that the overall school is required to meet. The overall school is reflected in the "all students" subgroup.

Understanding the term *subgroup* is key to understanding AYP and the accountability system of the State of Texas. In order to arrive at the AYP figures, the schools and school districts are evaluated through academic indicators. The indicators are tied to the outcomes within a particular subgroup. African American, Hispanic, White, and Economically Disadvantaged are the subgroups required for state accountability. Special Education and Limited English Proficient are added on the federal AYP requirement. Male and female indicators are added within each ethnic subgroup. All of the indicators point back to the success of a subgroup in their proficiency on the test.

By 2014 under the current AYP program, 100% of students in all categories must pass the state tests in order for a campus or district to meet AYP. Achieving AYP is the greatest challenge for all public schools as the 2014 mandate gets closer. If the AYP requirements are not lifted, the outcome is the inevitable sanctioning of each school district in Texas and across the country. This inevitable outcome will, in all likelihood, force the State of Texas into the federal waiver program. The trade-off for AYP standards being lifted is the acceptance of a new curriculum that is a national curriculum. The new national curriculum will bring new curriculum standards that every state will comply with, thereby syncing states together within one educational system. This is dealt with more in depth further in the study. (Note: As an update to clarify, the waiver was issued from the U.S. Department of Education and all school districts got a reprieve from the 100% mandate. The waiver, however, came with powerful strings attached as it was learned that the 100% mandate was only delayed, not removed.)

Cognitive Dissonance

The psychological implications associated with failure exemplify the impact on school culture and climate. With the impossible being asked, why are school districts going to any means to accomplish that which they know cannot be accomplished? One reason lies in understanding the obvious. Not to make a valiant attempt means certain failure and the possibility of state takeover, with the accompanying loss of autonomy in the operation of one's own school or school district. Another reason may lie at a much more subconscious level. Those educators who are in leadership positions have been in the education business for many years. They have grown up in the profession, and most have come to believe that the profession is moving forward toward greater and greater accountability, which translates into a meaningful education for the youth of today and the leadership of tomorrow. To think otherwise means that efforts made by educators over the last 50 years have been in vain and the system that is in place now is horribly flawed. By adopting this mind-set, educators are failing to understand the conditions they are asked to work within. When the impossible is asked and the consequence of failure is certain, the educator has a dilemma in his or her cognitive process to try to understand just what reality is unfolding. In order to mentally digest this conflict of reasoning, a process begins to unfold in the mind of the individual called *cognitive dissonance*. Cognitive dissonance is possibly at work in today's educators, whether they are teachers, counselors, principals, or superintendents. This psychological theory will be expanded in greater detail further into this study, but a basic understanding of the theory of cognitive dissonance is needed at this point.

Leon Festinger, an American psychologist, is known for his theory on cognitive dissonance.

> Festinger's (1957) cognitive dissonance theory suggests that we have an inner drive to hold all our attitudes and beliefs in harmony and avoid disharmony (or dissonance). Cognitive dissonance refers to a situation involving conflicting alteration in one of the attitudes, beliefs or behaviors to reduce the discomfort and restore balance etc. (McLeod, 2008, para. 1)

Cognitive dissonance plays a role in most people's fixed belief systems. Whether it is political leanings, religious constructs, the history of world events, or what is learned from textbooks and well-meaning teachers, people hold fast to beliefs that are set in their minds for many years. Sometimes these fixed beliefs are passed down for generations. Cognitive dissonance is explored further in depth to help with understanding the powerful forces at work in the human mind to keep personal emotions, belief systems, and cognitive reasoning all in sync. In failing to face the reality of the situation, the status quo is allowed to continue unabated toward its predetermined end result.

Theoretical Framework

To better understand the grounded theory that is presented in this study, discussion of the theoretical framework used for the theory is presented at this time. This study uses the theoretical framework of the Hegelian dialectic. Dialectic is the process of searching for the truth through opposing or contradicting paradigms (Raapana & Friedrich, 2005). Georg Wilhelm Friedrich Hegel is the German philosopher credited with encapsulating the dialectic, although the premise on which the dialectic is built predates Hegel and builds on the legacy of Immanuel Kant. Hegel was a friend and working associate of Friedrich von Schelling, another very influential philosopher of the day (European Graduate School, n.d.).

Hegel lived during a time of great philosophical enlightenment, when some of the greatest minds laid down a foundation of philosophy that is still built on today. Hegel lived from 1770 to 1831 and was alive to experience and be influenced by some of the greatest creative minds the world has ever seen. From this time period of expanded thought, such notables as Kant and Schelling were writing their philosophies. During this same period, Mozart and Beethoven were producing some of the greatest masterpieces in music. Hegel was 19 when the French Revolution broke out in 1789. His was a complex mind; he wrote books that influenced the world to this present day. He was a man of deep philosophical thought and intensity and is most noted for his dialectic of reason, which began with a thesis and progressed to an opposite, antithesis. This was then taken to a compromise that resulted in the synthesis. This new synthesis would result in a new thesis, and the process would continue working to a perfected state.

Two researchers who spent considerable effort in researching the connection between Hegel's dialectic and how the dialectic has played out in world events through the ages are Niki Raapana and Nordica Friedrich. According to Raapana and Friedrich (2005), it is Hegel's schematic of progressive action that leads from the initial problem and then results in an opposite reaction to the problem. Finally, a compromise to the original problem is agreed upon by both opposing forces and serves as the solution. The key in the dialectic (2005) is that those who created the problem managed the reaction and had the solution prepared before the problem was ever presented.

The Evidence Is Clear

What happened in the two neighborhoods used in this study symbolized the questionable nature of NCLB when played out to its end result. Much of the high stakes built into NCLB was beyond the school district to control. School administrators are bound by the law and must conform. When restructuring of a school is required, the district and school administrators have no choice but to comply with state agencies. When a restructure takes place, children from the ages of 5 through 18 have a different education format. If their neighborhood public school is turned into a public charter school, their attendance at the new public charter school is not guaranteed. They may need to apply or have their names placed into a lottery to determine where they will attend school. These newly created schools will have a new faculty and administration. Teachers and administrators who were previously at the schools will now be dispersed to other campuses in the school district. If, by chance, a parent's child is chosen to attend the newly restructured charter school (Whittaker, 2012), the parent will not have a voice in the operations of the school—not with the teachers, the curriculum, the daily schedule, or even the books that are in the library, if there is a library at the new school.

The method chosen for instruction is typically Outcomes-Based Education (Whittaker, 2012) or another title for the same style of instruction, Direct Instruction. Instruction and access to knowledge will come through the computer. The charter school administration is accountable only to the EMO or CMO that runs the school. Unless the public charter school is specifically working through the public school district that hired it for operations, there is not any elected official (school board trustee) to oversee the operations of the school that is accountable to the taxpayer. Some CMOs and EMOs operate within a school district with some district oversight, as previously discussed. In the case of a traditional public charter school, however, the taxpayer still pays school taxes, but has no voice in the pubic charter school his or her child attends. This represents taxation without representation, a problem of significance to those who believe in the United States Constitution.

Research Questions for Investigation

Laws written by the state and federal governments govern school operations and the education profession. School officials are charged with adhering to the laws that govern the operations of schools. There is no leeway for avoiding the law. In order to have clear questions to frame the data collection, I sought answers to the following important questions to guide the research study.

1. From the evidence presented, have the NCLB mandates served to propel schools and school districts toward AYP noncompliance?
2. What are the perceptions of parents toward the restructuring or closure of their neighborhood schools?
3. What are the perceptions of teachers and administrators who have been involved in the restructuring or school closure process?
4. What are the perceptions of parents of children affected through the restructuring of the neighborhood schools with regard to their representation in their taxation?

The Accountability Trap

Public schools are currently trapped in an endless spiral that is taking them further from the goals of academic achievement and into a morass of mediocrity. As long as the definition of an academically sound public school remains as it stands, that is, whether the public school "met standards" or "failed to meet standards", the academic outcomes will not change. Remember that meeting standards, according to the accountability system, is meeting the required percentages for each subgroup required for that school year. The punishment associated with failing to "meet standards", forces schools to stay in a continual state of preparation for the next test. This must change before any meaningful movement toward academic achievement is realized. This researcher's interest is to bring awareness to legislators, superintendents, and other public school stakeholders, as well as parents, so that the right questions may be asked. The interest of this researcher and the intent of the research contained in this study were also to present an awareness of the true condition of the public school accountability system as a system that should be eradicated. One result on a test designed by a professional test-developing company cannot give the educator a clear picture of the academic competence of a student. In speaking about the backlash from educators and activists against the policy contained in NCLB, Dr. Ravitch had these remarks:

> The problem is the misuse of testing for high-stakes purposes, the belief that tests could identify with certainty which students should be held back, which teachers and

principals should be fired or rewarded, and which schools should be closed—and the idea that these changes would inevitably produce better education. Policy decisions that were momentous for students and educators came down from elected officials who did not understand the limitations of testing. (Ravitch, 2010)

Perspectives in Philosophy

When I was developing the grounded theory for my dissertation, it was important that the element of truth lay at its foundation. This brought me to epistemology. In a discussion of epistemology, it is prudent to first define the topic. "Defined narrowly, epistemology is the study of knowledge and justified belief" (Stanford Encyclopedia of Philosophy, 2005, para. 1). With this definition in mind, *knowledge* and *justified* are words that require further exploration. Knowledge is only valuable and practical if it is true. False information serves no value except to confuse and mislead, and therefore cannot be correctly called knowledge. According to the Stanford Encyclopedia of Philosophy (2005), *justification* could loosely be described in this manner: "What *makes* justified beliefs justified? According to evidentialists, it is the possession of evidence" (2005, para. 4). An evidentialist is simply one who requires evidence to support belief. If a belief is justified, it has evidence that supports the justification.

For the purpose of this study, my research focused on the quest for *truthful knowledge* that is supported with *evidence* that justifies belief in the knowledge. My grounded theory had to be supported by truthful knowledge. It was safe to assume, therefore, that the findings in the data had to support the theory presented. This could only be determined after the evidence was accumulated in the findings of the data. Once the data were in place from the interviews, the theory would reveal itself as justified or unjustified. No Child Left Behind, to be credible, had to be supported by truthful knowledge that showed evidence in the improvement of the education system.

The Grounded Theory

The language in NCLB policy had an intended purpose behind the words used. The mandates that were made law requiring that 100% of the children in America be proficient in reading and math (as defined by the child's grade level) by 2014 posed an unrealistic, if not impossible, mandate to meet. Couple this with the elevation of difficulty on the assessment and the elevating of proficiency percentages for schools to reach each year, and the standards became more problematic. Add to all of these difficulties the withholding of funds by federal and state education agencies, which were meant to aid schools in accomplishing the mandated unrealistic tasks, and a pattern of obstruction begins to unfold. With these points in mind, the grounded theory postulated in this study was that No Child Left Behind was written with the intent of moving public schools to failure or weakening them to such an extent that the school officials would be forced to accept the waiver option proposed through the U.S. Department of Education and the Obama Administration. This was done so that a new, more prescriptive education system could emerge. The old system had to be torn down before the new system was revealed.

CHAPTER 3

A Carefully Crafted Agenda

The issue of evaluation is critical to the discussion of testing, technology, and the subjugation of the public school system in America by the federal government. One of the central complaints against the NCLB law is the punitive nature of the accountability system that is tied back to the student's performance on the test. The federal requirement, called Adequate Yearly Progress (AYP), is an increasingly difficult and unrealistic standard to meet. The AYP for each school is derived from a formula of passing percentages of the total student population on the standardized test, attendance rate for the school, and graduation rate for the school. Achieving an acceptable AYP rating is a difficult task now for some of the best academic public schools in America because the standards have risen to an unrealistic level. An explanation of this complex issue is needed to gain understanding.

The Specter of AYP

The student dropout rate is a significant factor for every high school. In Texas if students do not pass the yearly standardized state assessment, commonly called *the test*, by the end of their twelfth-grade year, they are considered a dropout, and they do not receive a high school diploma. An ongoing quest then unfolds: school officials must try to get students who have finished their high school curriculum and left the building to return and retake the test. Every school year, there is a designated test day in

October when high school counselors desperately try to convince former students to return to the campus and try again to pass the test. The former students hopefully agree to return and retake the test. If they pass, they get their high school diploma. If they don't pass, the process starts over again until passage is achieved or the student gives up. The student remains coded as a dropout until he or she passes the test. No longer is a Graduate Equivalency Diploma (GED) not counted against a school's dropout rate. If a student chooses to give up on the test and get his or her GED, he or she is still counted as a dropout. GEDs now affect the AYP of the school. In the eyes of NCLB, as each year goes by, more and more schools are failing due to not meeting Adequate Yearly Progress (AYP).

AYP failure places tremendous pressure on all professionals in education. Everyone feels pressure, and it flows downhill, beginning with the board of trustees and the superintendent. The necessity of making AYP and having a successful accountability rating has now manifested itself in the teacher's evaluation. The requirement for the teacher's evaluation to be tied to the students' test results forces teachers to devote their instructional time each day to testing strategies and elements that are traditionally seen on the test.

The Issue of Evaluation

Evaluations tied to test results were at stake in the Chicago teacher's strike of 2012. Accountability was the issue, and the measurement of accountability was tied to the test. There was also a question of sovereignty for the teacher. As an instructor, is there any room left for a teacher to be autonomous in any form with his or her instruction? Does all instruction have to come under one standard for all? Has the teacher become simply a conveyor of information handed down from on high by an "instructional specialist"? If this is the case, might a computer serve the same purpose? These are key issues involved in this study. As the issue of school closures due to failure to achieve AYP is addressed, the teacher as a purveyor of knowledge will also be addressed. The rules of instruction have changed, and at risk is the very nature of what it means to be a teacher.

The evaluation of teachers, as it relates to the state test, is not as straightforward as one might suppose. For the teacher's union in Chicago, discussed earlier, in order to achieve at least part of the issues in question, a compromise was needed with Mayor Emanuel. The teachers (McCune, 2012) received a 17.6% pay raise over the next three years, but they had to concede that at least part of their evaluation would be tied to outcomes on the standardized state test. Both sides had to give in order to get the children back in school, as is usually the case in strikes. The fear was that when the strike was over, the mayor would close many underperforming schools, thus laying off many union workers. When unions and politicians are involved, many hard-line issues become compromised so that work can commence.

Traditionally, teachers have been evaluated on what was observed by the evaluator in the same year. When evaluating teachers according to outcomes from the state test, the data can be difficult to judge fairly using criteria from the current school year's student scores compared to the scores from the previous year to establish a pattern of instruction. Consider the comments from a teacher interviewed for a dissertation by Barbara Woodward in 2011: "The data {are} always a little muddy when you're looking up students because you're not always comparing the same students. It's a problem because you're comparing last year's seventh graders to this year's" (Woodward, 2011, p. 111). This level of comparison would never be accepted as proof of accuracy in any other form of research data. Yet it is used every year to judge a teacher's worth and value. The practice of judging a teacher's effectiveness based on this evaluation system is questionable.

Technology, High-Stakes Testing, and the Rise of Public Charter Schools

This section will take a close look at technology, testing, and the link that each has with public charter school development. Technology will be explored from the standpoint of embedded curriculum as software used to teach the essential elements needed to pass the standardized test. In Texas, school districts have once again changed the structure of their essential elements to conform to a new state test—the State of Texas Assessment of Academic Readiness (STAAR). The testing conglomerate Pearson, Inc. develops each end-of-course test, not the teacher. The student's grade is affected by his or her testing outcome. The net result is to have huge implications for how the teacher chooses to instruct students.

The STAAR test's impact on the school is significant. With the passing percentage of the entire school now being lifted to an average of 92.5% and a new, more difficult end-of-course test being applied, superintendents and principals saw very difficult challenges for the 2012–2013 school year. Schools and school districts that were already in various levels of school improvement mandates by the Texas Education Agency due to not meeting their AYP standard saw little hope of achieving acceptability with the new higher percentages that were required. Superintendents across Texas and the United States are crying out for help. They are losing their schools. Schools that reached the maximum number of years of failure, which is five, are looking square in the face of restructuring by the Texas Education Agency (TEA). In some cases, entire school districts are in danger of takeover.

When a school reaches a point of failure where no further corrective measures can be applied, it is set up for restructuring. This is mandated through No Child Left Behind and carried out by each state's education agency. In Texas the entity that governs all public schools is the Texas Education Agency. Schools at the five-year maximum number of years for AYP failure have a few options for dealing with the failure. Leaving the school in its present state and choosing not to act is not an option. One option available for the school district is to contract with a Charter Management Organization (CMO) or an Education Management Organization (EMO) to manage the failed school and turn it into a public charter school. The CMO or EMO then usually turns the public school, or set of schools, into charter schools. The CMO or EMO then contracts with private providers for custodial, transportation, maintenance, cafeteria, and instructional personnel. The teachers that were formerly at the failed school are forced to resign and then reapply. Principals are also removed in favor of an administration selected by the CMO or EMO. In some school districts that are suffering not only from poor academic standards but also from devastating economic hardships, the entire school district is being outsourced. School districts in the Detroit area of Michigan, the New Orleans area in Louisiana, and some districts in Georgia opted to close operations and call in private contractors to run the former community schools. A case in point is Highland Park School District near Detroit.

> The public school district in this hard-luck city has come up with a radical answer for its troubled education system: It is outsourcing all of it. Highland Park School District, one of the state's lowest performing academically, says it will turn over its three schools and nearly 1,000 students to a private, for-profit charter school company—the second district in Michigan to take such a drastic step to avert financial collapse. The abrupt news last week sparked concern—and in some cases in the faded industrial city, which is nearly surrounded by Detroit. The parents came to hear from the charter company, Leona Group LLC, which promises to improve the learning environment and boost student performance in a district where only 22% of third graders passed state reading exams last school year and just 10% passed math. The results were even worse for high schoolers: about 10% were proficient in reading, and none in math. (Banchero & Dolan, 2012, para. 1–4)

Charter schools have been in existence long enough to provide a track record for evaluation of their effectiveness. By the end of the decade of the 1990s (Wohlstetter & Griffin, 1997), some charter schools were doing well and others were floundering. It was still unclear if the effort to put together charters was actually delivering a superior education when compared to public schools. Charter schools' effectiveness at providing a superior education for students needs to be established.

> Educational choice has also expanded through the growth of charter schools, which exhibit aspects of both public and private education. Charter schools are public because they are generally created or "chartered" by a governmental agency and rely on public funds for their operation. They must also follow certain legal requirements, such as testing their students for the No Child Left Behind Act (NCLB),

and not teaching religion. They are similar to private schools in that they may be free from requirements placed on public schools in such areas as choosing their student bodies and employing non-union teachers. They are mostly controlled by boards that are not publicly elected and managed by profit-making companies as well as non-profit entities. (Jennings, 2012, p. 4)

Jack Jennings, President and CEO of the Center on Education Policy, goes on to state from the findings on charter school overall effectiveness (2012) that students are not receiving a superior education when compared with public schools in the same neighborhoods. In fact, only 17% of charter schools produced higher test scores than comparable neighborhood public schools. Thirty-seven percent of charter schools (Jennings, 2012) produced scores that would be considered substandard to the public schools.

Worth noting is that charter schools do not appear to positively impact public schools in the same vicinity by improving public-school standards or innovations because charter schools are competing for students. According to a study by Buckley and Fisler (2002) comparing charter schools with public schools, this has always been one of the largest arguments used by politicians when they speak of offering school choice through charter school development or vouchers. Politicians have been adamant that if charter schools are promoted and encouraged to develop, then public schools would elevate their standards and produce better results. This is not correct information to disseminate to the public.

With findings such as these, one must wonder why such efforts for charter school development are continuing and why the U.S. Department of Education makes it such a cornerstone in its Race to the Top (RTTT) initiative. RTTT has in its requirement for application the provision that to qualify, states must have an aggressive charter school development program.

Most research studies agree that charter schools are, on average, no more successful than regular public schools; that evaluating teachers on the basis of their student's test scores is fraught with inaccuracy and promotes narrowing of the curriculum to only the subjects tested, encouraging some districts to drop the arts or other non-tested subjects; and that the strategy of closing schools disrupts communities without necessarily producing better schools. In addition, the "Common Core State Standards" in reading and mathematics that states must adopt if they hope to receive a waiver from the US Department of Education, have never been subjected to field-testing. (Ravitch, 2011, para. 9)

One has to wonder if the children of America are being used as subjects in an experiment designed to substantially change how education is delivered and assessed in America. Is the infusion of more technology in the form of hardware, software, and infrastructure expenditures at play in pushing more charter school development? These are guiding questions that were explored further by this researcher in the review of the literature.

The seeds for the subjugation, or takeover, of public school education were laid long ago in the 1930s. Charlotte Iserbyt, former Senior Policy Advisor in the Department of Education in the first Reagan administration, examined the documentation from the inside:

For those who wonder if the education change agents have introduced any new programs, methods or ideas during this last decade, the answer is 'No.' While we have a new title – No Child Left Behind – it is in fact the carefully planned agenda that was spelled out in a small book published by The American Historical Association. This book entitled *Report of the Commission on the Social Studies: Conclusions and Recommendations of the Commission* (Charles Scribner's Sons: N.Y., 1934) was funded by the Trustees of the Carnegie Corporation. Harold Laski, a professor of British Socialism, said of the Report: 'At bottom and stripped of its carefully neutral phrase the Report is an educational program for a socialist America.' The call for a socialist America, of course, requires that the school abandon traditional

academic 'teaching' and substitute 'workforce training'
or 'techademics' to accommodate the needs of a planned
economy. (Iserbyt, 2011, p.2)

Ms. Iserbyt, once again drawing from her firsthand experience within
the Department of Education, gives clues to the larger picture of why a
workforce is needed and why the schools in America are the perfect venue
for the development of the workforce.

In 1992 President George H.W. Bush signed the North
American Free Trade Agreement along with the President
of Mexico and the Prime Minister of Canada. Our
'industrial policy' was now in place. In 1993 the Heritage
Foundation of Washington, DC, home of many policy-
making new-conservatives, celebrated their twentieth year
of operation by publishing an annual report that featured
a congratulatory story about Richard Allen, a Heritage
policy analyst. 'The idea of the North American Free
Trade Agreement (NAFTA) originated with the Heritage
Fellow Richard Allen and has long been advocated by
Heritage policy analysts ... The idea of creating a North
American free trade zone from the Yukon to the Yucatan
was first proposed by Heritage Distinguished Fellow
Richard Allen in the 1970's, refined by then Presidential
candidate Ronald Reagan, and further developed in
a major 1986 Heritage Foundation study.' From 1994
forward, industry has vacated much of the United
States, leaving the job market bereft of entry-level jobs
for many Americans. In the meantime, the educational
establishment has continued to convert itself into a
workforce-training mode, even though there were going to
be no jobs available ... The agenda, initiated by Carnegie
Corporation in the early thirties and facilitated by the
United Nations Educational, Scientific, and Cultural
Organization (UNESCO), the Office of Economic and
Cultural Development (OECD), numerous tax-exempt

foundations, the U.S. Department of Education, the U.S. Chamber of Commerce and other governmental agencies has been implemented over the years to the tune of hundreds of billions of taxpayers' dollars. The first ten years of this century have seen full-speed implementation of the above Carnegie Corporation's totalitarian/socialist world government agenda. (Iserbyt, 2011, pp. 3–4)

A key point from this quote is that American governmental policy is written, not by members of Congressional committees, but by foundations and non-governmental organizations (NGOs) that have little oversight. NAFTA is just one example of these types of actions that have had huge implications for the country.

The increase in the use of technology is another planned operation that has as its target the implementation of a new style of teaching and a new curriculum for the children of America. The gradual increase in the use of technology in schools and the incremental increased use of standardized testing to judge a student's progress have a dual relationship that has worked as a detriment to America's schoolchildren. Both technology and the curriculum used in standardized testing have served to limit what the student learns to what is contained in the essential elements covered in the test.

In Texas these essential elements are called Texas Essential Knowledge and Skills (TEKS). Many education experts feel TEKS has led to a gradual dumbing down of America's school curriculum due to the TEKS relationship to those skills needed to pass the state test. In fact, Secretary of Education Arne Duncan alluded to just such a predicament during an interview for *The Hill's Congress Blog* by Emmanuel Touhey (2011). In this interview Secretary Duncan expressed the need to work together to solve the education system that has led to a "dumbing down" effect with our students. Duncan references when he ran Chicago schools and the difficulty he had in solving issues due to the strength of the teacher unions. He was looking forward to bringing a bipartisan effort into creating a system that values all subjects, including those that are not tested through standardized tests, like music, art, and drama. Secretary Duncan was decent to admit dumbing down, but without moving to illuminate the core of the problem that permits the dumbing-down effect, his words had minimal merit.

International Tests

Students in America have been on a gradual incremental path of education for the past 30 years because the education system has used the yearly standardized test as its measure of effectiveness. An examination of the overall effectiveness of testing, when compared on the world stage of education, should point out resounding success and domination, given the amount of time, energy, and money placed into the educational programs in the public schools. International tests such as the Third International Mathematics and Science Study (International Test Scores, n.d.) in 2011, involving a half-million students in 41 countries tested from grades 4, 8, and 12, found the U.S. children either in the middle of the other nations or dismally low. The international test scores of 2011 highlighted that the one exception was fourth-grade science, where the United States scored in fourth place. The United States being outshined by countries such as Hungary, Slovenia, the Czech Republic, and Bulgaria in the math scores was a real wake-up call for everyone associated with education in the United States.

> One would think that with vastly superior resources and the level of education spending which far exceeds these competitors we would out-perform nearly everyone-not so. Dr. Schmidt, who oversees the research effort into the TIMSS results, says the actual cause for the failures appears to be weak math and science curricula in U.S. middle schools. (International Test Scores, n.d., p. 2)

Another round of international testing from 2010 with a similar result is found in the OECD's Programme for International Student Assessment (PISA) competition. Angel Gurria, OECD's Secretary General, addressed the audience, which included Secretary of Education Arne Duncan. The top performers were Shanghai, South Korea, Hong Kong, Singapore, Finland, Canada, Japan, and New Zealand. The United States results were average at best.

Overall, the U.S. comes out as an average performer in reading (rank 14 in OECD) and science (rank 17), but the U.S. drops below the OECD average in mathematics (rank 25). Also, there is a very wide gap between the top 10% and the bottom 10% of 15-year olds in the U.S, similar to that observed between top and bottom performing PISA countries. (Gurria, 2010, para. 12)

The results from these international testing programs should not reflect poorly on the nation's middle schools. Each level of the education system is important, and each level should vertically align with the next level. Elementary school moving the students to a successful entry into middle school, and middle schools preparing the students for success at the high school level, is the intended format for the process. Each level is vital for the next. International comparisons, however, should always be viewed with some measure of skepticism. The variables that enter into comparisons of one country's school children when compared to another are so vast and different that straightforward comparisons are problematic. Still, the fact that the U.S. rank when compared with other countries has suffered in the last 20 years is noteworthy.

Increased Reliance on the Computer

With more and more of the teaching of the perceived essential elements coming through prescript software, the teacher is becoming more removed as the primary knowledge giver in the classroom. Dr. Dee U. Silverthorn gave the 2006 Claude Bernard Distinguished Lecture from the University of Texas at Austin. Dr. Silverthorn was reflecting on how teaching has changed at the university level from what he was accustomed to in the past.

Students have changed in the last 30 years as well. The generation of students we are now teaching grew up with computers. They have always known the Internet, videos, and CDs, but they may have never seen a typewriter. They laugh when you tell them that computers used to be larger than cars, because the students in the class of 2007 have always had computers that fit into their backpacks. What this means is that we are teaching a generation whose view of information access and transfer is totally different from that of their older instructors. When students today want to know about something, they are far more likely to Google it or go to Wikipedia than they are to pull down a book from a bookshelf. Every year when I talk to my students about finding scientific information, at least two-thirds of my juniors and seniors have never gone into the stacks in one of the University of Texas libraries to look for a book. What is more depressing for older scientists whose publications predate electronic indexing in PubMed is that for many students, if they cannot find information online, it might as well not exist. (Silverthorn, 2006, para. 5)

The point is well made by Dr. Silverthorn. The students no longer view the teacher as the academic authority in the classroom. Teachers are viewed as facilitators of the information. Information is seen to come from the computer. In the eyes of the students, the computer contains the information the student really needs. This can also be applied to the public school setting. The computer contains the information the student will need to access in order to pass the state assessment. With the added dimension of the teachers' evaluation tied to the students' test results, the teacher is forced to rely on the software in the computer to facilitate the learning for his or her students.

The seeds for the computer taking the place of the teacher were laid during the decades of the 1970s and 1980s. In Ms. Iserbyt's groundbreaking lifetime work *The Deliberate Dumbing Down of America* (1999), in which scores of documentation were catalogued and bound for the evidence to support the title of her book, a quote is referenced as taken from a 1984 book titled *Schooling and Technology, vol. 3, Planning for the Future: A Collaborative Model, An Interpretive Report on Creative Partnerships in Technology,* written by Dustin H. Heuston, PhD. Dr. Heuston is the founder of World Institute for Computer-Assisted Teaching (WICAT) and sees the computer as the answer to the age-old problem of the workload for the teacher being too burdensome. The fact that the teacher can use the computer to assist instruction and make the burden manageable is undeniable. However, it is when the computer is used in the affective domain to shape opinions and belief systems that the software in the computer becomes a powerful tool subject to misuse. In this quote, Heuston references the power the computer holds to mold and shape the minds of children while they are in school.

> We've been absolutely staggered by realizing that the computer has the capability to act as if it were ten of the top psychologists working with one student. ... You've seen the tip of the iceberg. Won't it be wonderful when the child in the smallest county in the most distant area or in the most confused urban setting can have the equivalent of the finest school in the world on that terminal and no one can get between that child and the curriculum? We have great moments coming in the history of education. (Iserbyt, 1999, p. 213)

Ms. Iserbyt remarked on this quote from Heuston,

> The comment regarding the computer's role as a "top psychologist" is as disturbing as is the idea of 'no one getting between the child and the curriculum.' These ideas lay to rest the publicly stated purpose of the words 'parent-school partnerships', which represent a superb example of semantic deception. (1999, p. 213)

The control of information and shaping of school children's minds are aided greatly through using the computer.

The trend in schools of replacing printed textbooks with computers is again feeding into the control of information through technology. The race to control the contracts for computer technology for schools is a multibillion-dollar business. The question of which company was going to get the contract to develop the new Common Core state assessments was settled. "One of the two consortia developing tests for the Common Core

State Standards has awarded a $12.5 million contract to Amplify Insight to develop a digital library of formative assessment professional learning tools for educators" (Cavanagh, 2013, para. 1). Further in Cavanagh's report, it is learned that the owner of Amplify Insight is Rupert Murdoch through his company News Corp.

> Amplify Insight is a division of Amplify, an ed-tech company whose chief executive officer is Joel Klein, the former New York City schools chancellor. Amplify is the education arm of the media conglomerate, News Corp., led by Rupert Murdoch. Last week, Amplify received a blast of media attention when it unveiled a new tablet device, loaded with classroom management tools and interactive lessons, at the South by Southwest education gathering. (2013, para. 4)

When it was revealed that Mr. Murdoch purchased Wireless Generation in 2010 (Phillips, 2010), which was the first company to be awarded a contract for the development of Common Core assessments (2010), and that Wireless Generation is now called Amplify, one begins to wonder what inside information may have been available for this acquisition. Of course, this is only a suspicion. Phillips goes on to reveal, "The company is likely to make a bid to build the technological pieces of the national tests that will be tied to the 'common core' standards" (2010, para. 9).

Mr. Murdoch reflected in this quote from his company's press release on the vast amount of money that it is possible to make in the education market. He also echoed the sentiment held by all of the entrepreneurs feeding at the trough of education with the children of America as guinea pigs, set up for experimentation.

> 'When it comes to K through 12 education, we see a $500 billion sector in the U.S. alone that is waiting desperately to be transformed by big breakthroughs that extend the reach of great teaching,' said News Corporation Chairman and CEO, Rupert Murdoch. 'Wireless Generation is at the forefront of individualized, technology-based learning

that is poised to revolutionize public education for a new generation of students.' (Phillips, 2010, para. 6–7)

Computers, software, testing, marketing, and grants, it all means big money for the business interests working to influence education policy makers.

State Assessments

The role of the standardized test as a unified state assessment of students and as a measure to evaluate the success of the student, the teacher, and the overall school is a lesson in gradualism. Incrementally the test has evolved, with each evolutionary step providing a more difficult measure. The series of tests implemented in Texas is not unique to Texas. Each state has had its own sequence of test evolution. In Texas this was a progressive series that began in 1980 with the Texas Assessment of Basic Skills (TABS). In 1985 a new test was developed, called the Texas Educational Assessment of Minimal Skills (TEAMS). An even more challenging test emerged in 1990 called the Texas Assessment of Academic Skills (TAAS). By 1992 it appeared that progress was being made. Student percentages of passing were increasing. Success looked attainable. It appeared that significant progress was being made in academic readiness by the late 1990s. It is important also to note (Combs, 2002) that school accountability, with publicized rankings and consequences for failure, began in Texas in 1993. It is critical to understand that TABS and TEAMS were utilized as assessments of minimal skills prior to TAAS. The prior standards were meant to indicate a level of functionality, not mastery of higher-order thinking skills. Beginning with TAAS, the test began to measure more than minimal skills. Still, however, the TAAS test was, by most school standards, a fair measure, where students could attain proficiency if given some adequate preparation.

In Texas on the TAAS test (Haney, 2001), the percentage of students passing the test jumped from 52% to 79% between 1994 and 1998. In 1997 Texas fourth graders (2001) made more progress on the National Assessment of Educational Progress (NAEP) than any other state in the country. While the academic achievement was noted, Haney's study went on to attempt to see the impact that the TAAS test was having attitudinally on the teaching profession and the students. Keep in mind that the TAAS test was the third installment in the state assessment and the most difficult one to date. Haney discussed the psychological impact of testing that was becoming "high stakes" for the school's accountability rating.

> These surveys were undertaken entirely independently (by Gordon and Reese; by myself and colleagues; and by Hoffman and colleagues), and surveyed somewhat different populations of educators. General findings from this review were as follows: Texas schools are devoting a huge amount of time and energy preparing students specifically for TAAS. Emphasis on TAAS is hurting more than helping teaching and learning in Texas schools. Emphasis on TAAS is particularly harmful to at-risk students. Emphasis on TAAS contributes to retention in grade and dropping out of school. Survey results indicated that the emphasis on TAAS is contributing to dropouts from Texas schools not just of students, but also teachers. In one survey, reading specialists were asked whether they agreed with the following statement: It has also been suggested that the emphasis on TAAS is forcing some of the best teachers to leave teaching because of the restraints the tests place on decision-making and the pressures placed on them and their students'. A total of 85% of respondents agreed with this statement. In another survey, teachers volunteered comments such as the following: 'Mandated state TAAS Testing is driving out the best teachers who refuse to resort to teaching to a low level test!' (Haney, 2001, p. 8)

As previously mentioned, the cognitive dissonance affecting the overall teaching establishment did not allow for the profession to truly zero in on what was actually occurring with their ability to instruct students in the manner they had become accustomed to. This was due to a steady increase in the call for school and teacher accountability that had been growing for a decade. President Clinton's Goals 2000 (Ravitch, 2010) had as one of its planks that states work to develop their own standards and develop tests that would measure a student's progress. The public was certainly behind these efforts due to continued erosion of faith in the public school system at large. By the time President George W. Bush came to Washington DC (Ravitch, 2010), the nation was looking for a miracle because of the progress reported from Texas with TAAS. When President Bush announced, with great fanfare, the 2014 mandate of 100% proficiency on the state assessment, it was met with little criticism. The public and the teaching profession were sufficiently conditioned to accept this unattainable goal.

The use of the word *proficiency* should in no way be confused with minimal skills or literacy. The term *proficiency* (Ravitch, 2010)—which is the goal of the law—is not the same as minimal literacy. The term *proficiency* has been used since the early 1990s by the federal testing program, the National Assessment of Educational Progress, where it connotes a very high level of academic achievement. President Bush was clever with the wording used at the time. Few understood or caught the significance of using the term *proficient*. The naivety of the educational profession not to realize what was meant by phrasing the dictate with the term *proficiency* led to little resistance. It most certainly set the stage (2010) for a continued rise in the difficulty of the assessment and the percentages required each year to reach 100% by 2014.

To reflect on the survey mentioned above from Haney (2001), it is worth repeating that despite showing some measure of success on the TAAS test, the fallout from the intense nature of preparation, benchmark testing, drills, and added pressure from administrators was a huge negative to the students and to the profession. So what did the Texas Education Agency (TEA), along with the Department of Education in Washington DC, do with this information? They developed an even more difficult test as the next evolution of the public school system in Texas and across the nation as part of the continued ramping up of accountability through NCLB. In 2003 TEA, along with Pearson Education, Inc. (AustInnovation, 2010), developed the Texas Assessment of Knowledge and Skills (TAKS). This test represented the most difficult measure for Texas students to date. It was so difficult, the developers of the test had to scale back the required passing percentages to give any school in Texas a reasonable chance of passing. With the TAAS test, the yearly passing percentage for students to gain a passing grade on the test was 70%. With the new TAKS system, due to the difficulty of the test, the passing percentage was lowered. But with each passing year, the percentage became higher. In like sequence, the school's overall passing percentage, to make AYP and the state accountability system, also went up with each passing year. Remember, the students must all become proficient by 2014.

The Role of Subgroups

Key in understanding the complexity of the accountability mandates is realizing that the overall student percentages of success are only one indicator by which the school and school district are evaluated. Enter the term *subgroup*. Every school and school district must have the percentages for AYP and the accountability rating met in each subgroup if the school or district is to be an granted acceptable ranking. The subgroups, to be counted in the overall ranking of the school, have to be at least 10% of the population of the school. The subgroups are listed as African American, Hispanic, White, Economically Disadvantaged, Limited English Proficient, and Special Education. For most schools it is possible for students in one subgroup to also be included in another subgroup, such as Economically Disadvantaged as well as the Special Education subgroup. This, of course, adds to the difficulty in meeting the percentages required. (Note: In Texas, as of 2014, the subgroups have expanded to include ten categories.)

A closer look at the special education dilemma faced by schools is needed to see the complexity of the issue of AYP. The guidelines of NCLB allowed for only 3% of the special education population to be exempted from the regular test. Other types of assessments were allowed for this 3% of special education students, demonstrating only a small percentage are sheltered in this manner. Most schools had a larger percentage than 3% of special education students sheltered from taking the regular TAKS test. With only 3% of special education students sheltered from the test, it created a very interesting development in most schools. Schools were now required to redistribute their special education students in regard to their placement and testing status. Resource classes that were taught at below grade level were dissolved, and resource students were now designated special education students with modifications and moved into regular education classrooms. The modifications referred to changes in the curriculum that were placed into the student's Individual Education Plan (IEP). The regular education teacher was then required to follow the student's IEP. (The reference to TAKS relates to Texas, and to the fourth installment of the standardized state test.)

The influx of more special education students into the regular education classroom put more of a strain on the regular education teacher. It took some time for teachers and students to adjust to this new situation. It also had a huge impact on the school's AYP rating. In the guidelines of accountability in NCLB, all demographic groups count separately in the accountability report. Special education students are categorized as a demographic group. In the accountability system, one subgroup can affect the entire school. Getting the special education subgroup to a passing level is often one of the most difficult challenges for an instructional team to accomplish. It virtually has the potential to set all schools up for failing marks.

The other subgroup that had the same potential to disrupt a schools chance to meet AYP standards were English Language Learner (ELL) students. Because of the difficult dynamics that ELL students had in getting through the language barrier, the challenge to pass the test proved sometimes extremely difficult.

Proficiency Percentages on the Rise

In order to get the schools to the point where all the students were passing the test by 2014, another embedded requirement of NCLB began to take place as the years progressed closer and closer to the deadline. As the passing rates increased, the percentage of total schoolchildren needed to pass to make AYP increased each year as well. In 2012 the school-wide passing percentage had climbed to 87% in Reading/ELA and 83% in Math. In other words, to make acceptable AYP standards, 87% of the students in each subgroup had to pass the Reading/ELA test and 83% of the students in each subgroup had to pass the math test. For 2013 the passing percentage was set to rise to 92% on Math and 93%

in Reading/ELA. The constant pressure to prepare the students for each round of testing was having an increasing negative impact on the teachers, counselors and administrators.

The Center on Education Policy (2010) conducted its own survey of results for schools not making AYP across the country. Their findings were for all public schools to not allow for population differentiation.

> The Center on Education Policy (CEP), an independent nonprofit organization, has been monitoring national AYP data going back to 2005. This spring, we updated the four-year trends described in our December 2010 AYP report by adding a fifth year of data on the estimated number of schools in the nation and each state that did not make AYP in 2010, based on tests administered in 2009-10. These data were collected from what we believe are the most reliable sources reported in the summer of a given year and are based on the results of tests administered in the school year that ended in the spring of that year. For example, AYP determinations for 2010 are based on test results from school year 2009-10. An estimated 38% of the nation's public schools did not make AYP in 2010. This marks an increase from 33% in 2009 and is the highest percentage since NCLB took effect. In 12 states and the District of Columbia, at least half of the public schools did not make AYP in 2010. In a majority of the states (39 and D.C.), at least one-fourth of the schools did not make AYP. (Center on Education Policy, 2010, para. 2)

Linking the Teacher to the Test

The latest evolution of testing in Texas is called the State of Texas Assessment of Academic Readiness (STAAR). This is an end-of-course exam testing the student's knowledge of the course he or she is taking at the time. The STAAR is to be given in Language Arts and Math through grade 5, with Language Arts, Math, Science, and Social Studies being administered in middle school and high school. Preliminary indications are that this latest installment is the most difficult evolution of the state test to date. With school failure a certainty, President Obama issued his waiver plan to the states and provided relief for schools across the country.

Returning for a moment to the Chicago teachers' strike, the main issue with the teachers and the union representing them, the American Federation of Teachers (AFT), was the evaluation system. With more and more schools, and now entire school districts, being replaced by charter schools, teachers see their livelihood at stake. The entire profession is an endangered species, and the teachers' union is trying to divest itself from the accountability system that ties teachers' job security to a system for evaluating schools based on testing outcomes.

Testing is a key issue in the debate, and the use of technology needs to be examined as well. Technology is worthy of a closer look because it is the primary disseminator of information in charter schools. The use of the computer as the primary instructor is tailor-made for a school system that bases its instruction through a series of courses that present coursework in the form of computer programs for the students to matriculate. The Chicago teachers know what is at stake, and they are taking a stand to protect their profession.

> At Lane Tech College Prep, where many passing motorists honked their support for the teachers, Steve Parsons, a teacher, said he believed the city was ultimately aiming to privatize education through charter schools and computer programs that teach classes online. 'We need to stay out as long as it takes to get a fair contract and protect our schools,' he said. (Davey, 2012, para. 17)

The settlement in the strike included tying evaluations to the outcomes of the tests. The teachers got the pay raise but lost on the issue of evaluation linked to the testing outcomes. This is important, for if the state is to control what is taught, the instruction must be linked to the essential elements of the test and the teacher must be evaluated on his or her students' outcomes on the test. The Chicago teachers made a statement that the rest of the nation heard, but in the end, their evaluations will still be linked with the student testing outcomes.

Common Core State Standards

When I first began writing my dissertation in 2012, new national curriculum standards were being developed for states to accept in order to receive the waiver to the AYP standards of NCLB. "On September 23, 2011, President Obama formally outlined the Administration's comprehensive ESEA flexibility package, which will grant states waivers from specific provisions of NCLB/ESEA in return for their agreement to implement certain reform measures" (Center on Education Policy, 2011, para. 3). The centerpiece of the waiver agreement is the Common Core State Standards, sometimes referred to as CCSS and other times simply as Common Core. It is the new national standards, and it will place every state under the same education standards. The Common Core State Standards (Common Core) marks a new development in the ever-increasing expanse of the federal government into what, heretofore, has been the sole responsibility of the states. The use of federal funds (in the form of Race To The Top grants or acceptance of the waiver) to establish grade-level standards that the states must follow is a new development with huge implications. If the states apply and get accepted into the waiver system, one of the main provisions of receiving the waiver is to accept the federal funds to establish the Common Core standards in all the schools. This has never been done before because provisions were written into NCLB to prevent this from happening.

> Despite three federal laws that prohibit federal departments or agencies from directing, supervising or controlling elementary and secondary school curricula, programs of instruction and instructional materials, the U.S. Department of Education ("Department") has placed the nation on the road to a national curriculum, according to a new report written by a former general counsel and former deputy general counsel of the United States Department of Education. (Gass, 2012, para. 1)

In fact, the NCLB policy states in subpart one of section 1111, State Plans, Part A—Improving Basic Programs Operated by Local Education Agencies, as follows:

> (A) Each State plan shall demonstrate that the State has developed or adopted challenging content standards and challenging student performance standards that will be used by the State, its local educational agencies, and its schools to carry out this part, except that a State shall not be required to submit such standards to the Secretary. (U.S. Department of Education, n.d.,b. p. 1)

Referring to the study performed by the Pioneer Institute, it explained:

> 'The Department has designed a system of discretionary grants and conditional waivers that effectively herds states into accepting specific standards and assessments favored by the Department,' said Robert S. Eitel, who co-authored the report with Kent D. Talbert. The authors find that the Obama administration has used the Race to the Top Fund and the Race to the Top Assessment Program to push states to adopt standards and assessments that are substantially the same. 'By leveraging funds through its Race to the Top Fund and the Race to the Top Assessment Program, the Department has accelerated the adoption and implementation of the Common Core State Standards ("CCSS") in English language arts and mathematics, as well as the development of common assessments based on those standards,' added Talbert, former General Counsel of the Department. 'Proponents of national standards, curriculum and tests claim they're merely a logical extension of previous federal education initiatives,' said Pioneer Institute Executive Director Jim Stergios. 'The key difference is that prior to Race to the Top and the recently announced federal waivers, the U.S. Department of Education abided by statutes explicitly

prohibiting federal direction, supervision, or control of curricula or instruction.' (Gass, 2012, para. 4)

Explored further by Jaime Gass, in her Pioneer Institute study, is how the waiver policy directs school districts toward a national curriculum standard. In order to obtain the waiver from the U.S. Department of Education, the states have to show evidence that they are adopting standards that prepare students for college or a career and are common from state to state. This is where Common Core found its name. The adoption of the Common Core State Standards (CCSS) will bring yet another round of training and learning a new system, complete with professional development demands on teachers and new approaches in learning styles for students.

> Adoption of the CCSS is merely the first step. Advocates envision that the standards will guide teaching and learning and help ensure that students receive a consistent, high-quality education. For this to occur, however, states and school districts, as well as teachers and school leaders, must make complementary changes in curriculum, instruction, assessment, teacher professional development, and other areas. (Center on Education Policy, 2012, p. 1)

In Texas, until such time as the TEA and the state government accept some provision for escaping the 2014 mandate, it will have to be assumed that school districts will fail, one by one, to make AYP and realize the necessity of accepting President Obama's waiver option. Many school districts that thought this idea unthinkable in the past are now looking down the barrel of restructuring their schools and, eventually, whole districts. The number of school districts that escape unscathed this year will be very few, if any. Once a school in Texas has five years of not making AYP in the same subgroup, it is in line for restructuring through TEA. This is what makes accepting the waiver inevitable. Otherwise, more schools fail and more restructuring is needed in order to comply with the law of NCLB. The more restructuring that is needed, the more school districts may choose public charter schools as the route to take in their restructuring efforts.

If the public charter school route is taken, only a percentage of students who attended the school will be accepted into the new public charter school. Usually none of the teachers are brought back, nor the administration. All teachers and administrative personnel, if under contract, are relocated to jobs elsewhere in the district. Students that are not accepted to the new restructured charter school will be bused to other schools in the same district as enrollment allocations allow.

On the east side of Austin, Texas, this has become a reality for the parents of the schoolchildren and the school employees who worked in the schools that have reached AYP failure. In the case involving Allan Elementary, the selection of students to attend the newly formed charter elementary school worked differently than a traditional lottery. The focus of the problem on the east side of Austin was the high school. AYP failure was a part of the high school academic difficulties for many years. The CMO, which contracted with the city (Whittaker, 2012), preferred to take schools in a block that forms the feeder pattern for the high school. This made Allan Elementary the first school slated for charter management. Allan Elementary was academically sound; it met AYP standards. The charter management company convinced Austin ISD officials that if the high school were to improve it would only do so over time with the schoolchildren rising up through the ranks under the guidance and leadership of the CMO. The parents in the community had made it clear to Austin ISD they did not intend to send their children to a charter school. When Allan Elementary was turned into a charter school, it was forced to look for children outside the attendance zone to fill the school due to the neighborhood parents opting out. The parents chose to send their children to other elementary schools in the same east side section of the city. This action by the neighborhood parents, to take a stand against charter schools, put them at odds with Austin ISD and set in motion a series of events that resulted in a change in school board members and the eventual ouster of the charter management company hired by Austin ISD.

The Computer as the Teacher

In public charter schools (Taylor, 2010), the computer is the preferred tool for instruction. The teacher is the facilitator for the computerized, individualized instruction of the student. In the case of KIPP schools, in order to control expenditures, veteran teachers were replaced with Teach for America teachers, and most recently many teachers were replaced with computers. "First KIPP was replacing qualified and certified teachers with Teach for America, Inc. (TRA) recruits with five weeks of training; now it's cutting costs by adding computers and subtracting teachers" (2010, para. 3). For the public charter school, it comes down to finances, with the computer being considered as more financially viable than the teacher. In fact, this is the wave of the future of economic concerns because teachers are considered an economic liability for public schools. Teachers are seen as a financial liability with national economic conditions not showing signs of improvement. It is fast becoming the trend to replace (Ferenstein, 2011, para. 1) selected faculty with computers and have the remaining teachers serve more as facilitators of instruction. In fact, it was reported that if this trend continues, the teaching profession, as we know it, might soon be extinct. The report states, "as long as schools measure performance simply by rote memorization on multiple-choice tests, no teacher can compete with instant access to the world's information. Unless schools change, more and more teachers will find themselves replaced by computers" (para. 3). Note the comment about rote memorization on multiple-choice tests. This is an example of the dumbing-down effect. Rote memorization that is used for a test and is not part of a daily drill that is followed, with continued application that becomes permanently imprinted in the brain (such as multiplication tables), is usually forgotten.

Outcomes-Based Education

As mentioned in chapter two, the actual method of instruction that best fits into this test-centered, computer-based system of education is Outcomes-Based Education (OBE). In order to obtain a measured, objective standard that schools and students are measured by, education experts have turned to Outcomes-Based Education methods. The key to understanding OBE is that it is a system of instruction that places the emphasis on student outcomes, rather than the available resources placed in front of the student that would be categorized as *inputs*. Knowledge is measured and defined prior to the instruction. That which is not tested is not valued. It is considered excess. Time and talent are defined within the scope of what is valued through measurement. Evaluation is measured through outcomes performed through examination.

Again, OBE is perfect for instruction that is built around a computer. Software can be developed around standards previously defined. Students gain advancement in the programs through a stimulus-response type of program that rewards the student when he or she gives the correct answer. The program also causes students to repeat and stall advancement if they answer incorrectly. In fact, virtually all credit recovery course work is built around advancing students at their own pace until they work their way through the course work and receive credit for the course.

What is the result of this increased use of the computer as the method of instruction? The interaction of the teacher giving way to interaction with *the box* will undoubtedly have a profound impact on the student. Increased computer use is part of a plan to restructure the school system through the practice of charter schools replacing public schools in a public/private endeavor, which is becoming more common as more schools reach the failure point in their attempts to reach acceptable levels of AYP. The computer is a necessary tool for this program due to the software that is used to implement the new public charter schools and the adoption of the Common Core State Standards curriculum that will soon be used by all schools under the waiver.

Charlotte Iserbyt, considered an expert in the prescript nature of OBE due to its predetermined standards and performance-based approach to learning, explains how OBE is increasingly applied in the NCLB era to the point that all instruction is now OBE. Anything in the school system that is not tested is not valued. In Iserbyt's quote we get a glimpse into the larger picture of why school choice and public charter schools are so important to the power brokers in education.

The choice proposals being recommended by most state Governors will ultimately destroy all forms of education: public, home school, private, and religious. The most lethal form of education choice is tax-supported private schools (charter schools), which have no elected school boards resulting in 'taxation without representation.' This is an oppressive system (taxation without representation), which caused our nation to revolt and declare war against the British (the American Revolution, 1776). What is to keep Americans from accepting the unelected council form of government at all levels of government, once one of the major sections of our economy (education) is being run by unelected councils? Do Americans think giving up their representative/elective form of government is a good idea? I doubt it." (Iserbyt, 2012, para. 10)

Vouchers

Charlotte Iserbyt's comment (2012) that refers to all forms of education—public, private, homeschooled, or religious—refers to the use of government tax-related funds moving from public to private education. Once federal money is used, federal oversight is imposed. This is the deceptive nature of the voucher program. The idea that parents are receiving a choice in the education provided for their children is part of the deception used by conservatives and liberals alike in government. The *choice* the parents receive will only invite federal government oversight, which will shackle the private school in the same manner it has the public school. Mrs.Iserbyt (2002) recognized this immediately after the Supreme Court decision that declared school vouchers constitutional.

Let me warn parents and private school administrators: "Freedom to choose" is exactly the opposite of what they and the private sector will receive if they take one penny of federal, state, or local tax money to educate children. Believe it or not, slavery is right around the corner, since once the private sector is controlled through vouchers, thereby creating a partnership with government (corporate fascism), students, having been psychologically profiled, will be tracked into specific training at an early age and later into job slots to suit the needs of the corporate sector and the global economy. (Iserbyt, 2002)

The Supreme Court decision in *Zellman v. Simmons-Harris* was the catalyst that legally set vouchers as constitutional and upheld other voucher movements in other states. "The court's decision confirms that the ability to choose the best school available, be it public or private, is a freedom that should be enjoyed by all Americans, not just those who can afford it" (Mass, 2002). This quote was given after the Supreme Court decision in July 2002 that awarded Ohio's Pilot Project Scholarship Program legal right to continue (Legal Information Institute, 2002). The program at the time was offering tuition aid for qualifying students in the Cleveland City School District. The choice of which private school to attend was the decision of the parent.

In what President Bush hailed as a "landmark ruling" and a victory for the American family, the Supreme Court Thursday ruled that a school voucher program in Cleveland does not infringe upon the constitutional separation of church and state. In a 5-4 ruling, the Supreme Court said the school voucher program does not constitute the establishment of religion. The much-anticipated ruling on the pilot project involving inner-city Cleveland schools came on the final day of the Supreme Court term, which began in October. (Frieden, 2002)

As Mrs. Iserbyt (2002) points out, once the money is accepted, the private institution ceases to be private. The voucher program is an alternative that is supported by members of both political parties. With both parties working in tandem and the Supreme Court being a willing participant, all that is left is for states to find ways to eliminate traditional public schools through the state houses of government, and the voucher program will be nationwide.

Continuity of Agenda

In 2012–2013, school districts were faced with an impossible task, that is, bringing every student to a point where he or she could pass the state assessment. Currently, in 2014–2015, they are still on the path to attain perfection in testing. This will be discussed in chapter 5.

The consequences of NCLB (Orange, 2012) have been devastating. High school dropout rates have increased (2012); many schools subsequently narrowed their curriculum focus to only the tested subjects, and with increased emphasis on teacher evaluation tied to the test, more teachers now teach to the test. The federal government imposed a difficult mandate (all students will be proficient) and framed the accountability picture within the parameters of this mandate. This virtually assures that all school districts will eventually come under the guidance or control of the federal government and the U.S. Department of Education. Consider this quote on AYP progress, written shortly after the passage of NCLB.

> Bills passed by the U. S. House of Representatives and the U.S. Senate in spring 2001 to reauthorize the Elementary and Secondary Education Act (ESEA) not only reinforce but strengthen the education accountability provisions contained in the Improving America's Schools Act (IASA) of 1994. Title I of the IASA requires states to establish challenging content and performance standards, implement assessments that measure student performance against these standards, and hold schools and school systems accountable for the achievement of all students. Specifically, states and local school districts must determine whether schools and school districts are making adequate yearly progress (AYP) in bringing students up to state standards, identify for school improvement any school that does not make adequate yearly progress for two consecutive school years, target resources to these schools, and, if necessary, take corrective action. The IASA calls for AYP to be defined in a manner that (1) results in continuous and substantial yearly improvement

of each school and local education agency sufficient to achieve the goal of all children ... meeting the state's proficient and advanced levels of achievement; [and] (2) is sufficiently rigorous to achieve that goal within an appropriate timeframe (As cited in Elmore and Rothman, 1999, p. 85). (Goertz, n.d., p. 1)

The Improving America's Schools Act (IASA) was passed in 1994, eight years before NCLB would make AYP a household name among school administrators and teachers. This demonstrates the seamless continuity of agenda that exists in government. One administration flowing into the next, no matter which party is in power, seems to be more the rule than the exception.

In 1965 at the inception of the Elementary and Secondary Education Act (ESEA), President Lyndon Johnson was in office, and he was a member of the Democratic Party. The next president, Richard Nixon, was a Republican, and he kept the status quo. Presidents Gerald Ford (Republican), Jimmy Carter (Democrat), Ronald Reagan (Republican), George H. W. Bush (Republican), and Bill Clinton (Democrat) followed in succession. All of these presidents allowed ESEA to continue basically unchanged. Each president may have had his own twist to the policy, such as President Clinton's Goals 2000, but these were just adaptations to the ESEA bill without major changes. Following President Clinton, the next president of the United States was President George W. Bush, a Republican. Under President Bush, ESEA was reauthorized, and No Child Left Behind was born. NCLB greatly expanded the federal government's authority over education and implemented the IASA of 1994, writing into law the AYP federal accountability. As with his predecessors, President Bush did not create a new education policy; he expanded on what was already in place. The end result was even greater authority of the federal government over what was once the state's jurisdiction and authority. Finally, President Barack Obama (Democrat) has kept all of ESEA and NCLB in place and has added his own twist to the policy. President Obama's education stamp is Race to the Top (RTTT), which is competition between states for federal money based on a number of items that focuses on effective measures to raise student test scores.

Once again, the federal programs already in place are not removed. Instead, they are expanded. ESEA and NCLB are held in place, and RTTT only serves to cement the federal authority through competition for federal dollars that make states more dependent on the federal government. The federal mandates that force school districts to spend additional dollars to meet AYP standards continue to divert funds into professional development and computer software programs to try to come up to mandated standards.

All of this was made possible by the initial passage of ESEA and the state's acceptance of federal money. The federal money did bring some good programs to the public schools. It also made the locally controlled, state-operated school districts forever addicted to the money to continue the programs. New laws were passed, such as the Individual with Disabilities Education Act (IDEA), which created new mandates and policies that states had to follow if the money was going to continue to flow to the local school districts. With each election, nothing was done to stop this ever-encroaching expanse of federal control. It marched along from one administration and congressional election to the next. Who can argue against providing needed funding for schools located in areas of extreme poverty? Obviously an argument cannot be made for schools being better off without these programs. What can be said against providing much-needed funding for disadvantaged, disabled schoolchildren? Of course, nothing can be said to refute the good that has been done through IDEA (Individual with Disabilities Education Act). As the federal programs became mandated, however, it forever tied the local and state education agencies to the federal arm and paved the way for more mandates to come. Once the programs are started they can't be stopped.

Federal Encroachment

In order to have public acceptance of ESEA and NCLB, it was necessary for points in the programs to have merit that worked for the betterment of students. ESEA and NCLB have set in motion some policies that have been favorable for children. The entitlement programs initiated through ESEA, especially Title I, have been beneficial in leveling the playing field for students that are disadvantaged. NCLB has done a service by forcing school districts to pay attention to segments of the student population that were not receiving adequate attention. Title I and IDEA were two federal initiatives, however, that forever tied the states education programs to the federal government. More policies were to come and with each new policy came a heavier hand of federal control.

The accountability system that came in Texas with TAAS, and the AYP system that was initiated through NCLB, greatly changed the direction of each school's academic focus. Both systems focused the responsibility for student failure on the school. This was very significant. *Accountability* is a word that is used often in today's society. When the word *accountability* was injected into the school model, it brought with it the responsibility to find ways to make students successful. In today's education system, that means passing the state assessment. With each passing year and higher percentages required of student mastery, the focus shifted away from the student and what he or she did or did not do to perform to make the grade deserved, and focused now on what the teacher did not do in terms of instruction and what the school did not do in terms of supplying the necessary tools for the teacher to ensure student success. When student success was not achieved to the necessary degree to achieve AYP compliance, sanctions and penalties followed. When the 2014 date become more of a reality for educators, teachers began to feel the pressure applied by principals and central office personnel in greater degrees, all with the evidence beginning to mount that the goal of all students achieving proficiency by 2014 would not be realized.

School Closures

As the 2014 deadline for 100% proficiency approached it became clear that the mandates would not be met; yet the standards remained in place. School failure continued, and school closures continued to disrupt communities. (Note: by 2015 schools all over the country are on a new, but different path to the same 100% mandate. This is explained further in the book.) School districts in virtually every major city in the United States are closing schools. Examples from Philadelphia, Chicago, and Houston will be addressed in this section. The Philadelphia School District is a perfect example of an urban district in crisis due to a large budget deficit. It is addressing its problem by shutting down underperforming and under populated schools. "Officials facing a $1.35 billion spending gap over five years are set to vote tomorrow on a proposal to shut almost 12 percent of Philadelphia's public schools" (Varghese, 2013, para. 2). The closings, though, have as much to do with a drop in municipal bonds and credit ratings as they do with underperformance from AYP failure.

> This really helps them deal in the short term to get their budgets more and more in balance, which is usually good for credit ratings and potentially good for spreads as well, said Paul Brennan, a senior portfolio manager at Chicago-based Nuveen Asset Management." (2013, para. 5)

As is the case in other cities where schools are shut down, public charter schools move in to take their place. The net result of savings to a school district is minimal. "The district of about 205,000 students isn't alone in shuttering facilities as enrollment falls while the percentage of students attending publicly financed charter schools almost triples" (Varghese, 2013, para. 6). The rise of public charter schools in the Philadelphia School District is part of the problem. As more charters are opened, funds are diverted from the district budget to fund the charters since charters are tax-supported entities. To add to the budget deficit, state funding for annual enrollment figures in the public schools drops as well. As more students move from the public schools into the charter schools, the Philadelphia School District budget gets hit from both sides: state allocations for ADA (average daily attendance) and required funding for charter schools.

> The rapid growth of charter schools, which now enroll close to 30% of the district's 200,000 students, have emptied approximately one-quarter of the seats in the district's school facilities since 2003, as shown in the exhibit below (exhibit not available). The growing number of students in charter schools has created an imbalance between the state aid the district receives and the number of schools it maintains, creating overcapacity in district-managed schools. (Distefano, 2013, para. 9)

The report continues, "In addition, because the district is required to provide funding for district students attending charters schools on a per-pupil basis, a growing portion of its aid revenues have been redirected towards charter schools over the past decade" (Distefano, 2013, para. 10). The paradox is hard not to recognize. On the one hand, Philadelphia School District is telling its parents and taxpayers that it has to close schools due to underpopulated buildings and low performance, and on the other hand, it is diverting much of the funds saved from the closings to charter school openings.

In Chicago there are similar happenings with school closures, this time closing 50 elementary schools plus hundreds of teachers dismissed for poor performance. The cuts are the largest in the country to date. This report out of Reuters (Young & Kelleher, 2013, para. 1) is as of March 2013. "Thousands of demonstrators rallied in downtown Chicago on Wednesday to protest the city's plan to close 54 public schools, primarily in Hispanic and African American neighborhoods." The report goes on to speak about the shortfalls in the budget and how the closings are a cost-saving measure for the city. "The public school district, the third largest in the United States, has said it has a $1 billion annual deficit and needs to close under-used schools to save money. It believes the plan will save $560 million over the next decade" (Young & Kelleher, 2013, para. 5). With the school closures comes an increase in the number of charter schools that are planned, which are tax-supported and which will require budgeted funds to operate.

"An expansion of charter schools is at the heart of the school closings debate in Chicago. Charter schools are publicly funded, but mostly non-union and their numbers have increased even as neighborhood public schools are closed" (Young & Kelleher, 2013, para. 18). Bearing in mind that one of the criteria to receive Race to the Top funds is an aggressive public charter school development program, one has to wonder if districts are positioning themselves to bring in large amounts of federal dollars through the creation of public charter schools at the expense of the children who attend the traditional neighborhood schools.

In Houston, the North Forest Independent School District, located just north of the city of Houston, has struggled for years with underperformance issues. The measuring criteria used to judge performance are important to remember when discussing underperformance. They are the standardized state tests and federal AYP accountability standards. Equally important to keep in mind is that urban school districts are the hardest hit with AYP due to social conditions related to poverty. To automatically declare that North Forest ISD is an academically inferior district that warrants closure is a gross miscarriage of justice for all of the teachers, counselors, and administrators that have worked tirelessly to try to reach acceptable AYP. The new State Commissioner Michael Williams has made the decision to close North Forest ISD, sending the entire district into the Houston Independent School District. Many of the school buildings will remain open, but they will be under new management beginning July 2013.

> Commissioner of Education Michael L. Williams today notified representatives of the North Forest Independent School District (NFISD) of his formal recommendation to close the NFISD and annex it into the Houston Independent School District (HISD), effective July 1. Williams based his decision on the district's continued poor academic performance over the past year as reflected in its low high school completion rate and poor performance on statewide assessments. (Texas Education Agency, 2013c)

Placing a label of poor performance on the students is shortsighted and a clear demonstration of catering to a standard of measurement that has been proven to not be indicative of true performance and proficiency. It is a judgment made with only one criterion, a standardized test outcome. Consider the phrasing used by Commissioner Williams:

> 'The decision to close a school district is a tough decision for all involved but we can no longer be tolerant of chronic underperformance,' said Commissioner Williams. 'My recommendation is based on the district's poor performance over the past year, which is reflective of a familiar pattern of failing to meet student needs over decades.' (Texas Education Agency, 2013c)

Commissioner Williams continues, trying to placate the employees of NFISD:

> 'I fully recognize that there have been people in North Forest ISD working hard to turn things around for a very long time, but we can no longer afford to wait,' said Commissioner Williams. 'More importantly, the students of North Forest can no longer afford to wait for a strong education they need and deserve.' (Texas Education Agency, 2013c)

In defense of Commissioner Williams, he met his legal responsibility under NCLB, which provides options for restructure. When options tried over the years prove unsuccessful, closure is inevitable. NCLB law stipulates that after five years of failing to meet AYP standards, action must be taken to restructure. If failure continues, the state steps in to close the school. In the case of North Forest, the state closed the entire school district. In an update to this situation reported on June 29, 2013 (Lodhia, 2013), North Forest ISD lost its appeal to Commissioner Williams to grant it more time to solve its accountability issues. North Forest ISD was closed and officially moved under Houston ISD's operations and oversight beginning with the 2013–2014 school year.

Facing Reality

Professor Linda Darling-Hammond realizes that perhaps this education system that evolved over the last 30 years is not something to hold up as an example of quality education. Dr. Darling-Hammond has been at the forefront of education reform for years, and she helped to develop the Interstate New Teacher Assessment and Support Consortium (INTASC) licensing standards for new teachers. She has worked on many blue-ribbon panels looking for solutions to the country's education woes. President Obama had her as a finalist for his selection of Education Secretary, deferring instead to Arne Duncan. To say that Linda Darling-Hammond is an insider in the world of education is an understatement, at the very least. She was part of President Obama's team of education advisors and is intricately involved (Klonsky, 2011) in the promotion of the Common Core State Standards. Darling-Hammond made comments about the state of the public school systems in America (2011), and her comments caught people's attention. Perhaps Dr. Darling-Hammond was finally coming around to a new paradigm in her thinking about where the system has been and where it is going.

At the Save Our Schools rally in Washington DC in March 2011, Dr. Linda Darling-Hammond had these comments:

> It is not acceptable to have schools in our cities and poor rural districts staffed by a revolving door of beginning and often untrained teachers, many of whom see this as charity work they do on the way to a real job. And it is not acceptable that the major emphasis of educational reform is on bubbling in Scantron test booklets, the results of which will be used to rank and sort schools and teachers, so that those at the bottom can be fired or closed – not so that we will invest the resources needed actually to provide good education in these schools. We are here to challenge the aggressive neglect of our children. With 1 out of 4 living in poverty— far more than any other industrialized country (nearly double what it was 30 years ago); a more tattered safety net – more who are homeless, without health care, and without food security; a more segregated and inequitable system of public education, in which the top schools spend 10 times more than the lowest spending; we nonetheless have a defense budget larger than that of the next 20 countries combined and greater disparities in wealth than any other leading country. (Strauss, 2011, para. 5)

Dr. Darling-Hammond, after years of living in the trenches of school reform, now may understand the achievement gap is not about test scores; it is about equity in funding for school districts and proper, meaningful measures to eradicate poverty. Any efforts short of meeting those two items will fall hopelessly to the floor in failure. Consider Dr. Darling-Hammond's thoughts on this subject:

> How many studies must be done before policy-makers understand that supportive early learning environments are critical, that teachers and education leaders must be well-trained and well-supported, that any effort to close the achievement gap is doomed to fail if we don't equitably fund all schools and properly staff them? (Strauss, 2010, para. 19)

In the North Forest ISD north of Houston, Texas, where poverty is a central issue that works against the hard work of teachers in their schools, the endgame of NCLB was realized with the loss of their entire school district. The same can be said of Philadelphia, Chicago, and every urban school district in America. They may not have lost their entire district, but significant numbers of schools have been lost to the mandates of AYP and NCLB. For the North Forest ISD, poverty and its accompanying effects are major factors affecting standardized testing outcomes. People were told that schools were being closed due to *academic failure* and *low performance standards*. Yet many educational professionals questioned this approach. These schools have closed because they were targeted schools, set up to fail by a system impacted by poverty and economic disequilibrium. The urban minority, poverty-ridden schools are easy prey for those who wish to take advantage of issues of poverty and lack of funds. The mechanism was created for takeover. The mechanism is the AYP accountability system. It was codified into law. The AYP accountability system set impossible standards that made failure a planned inevitability, and now the schools stand ready to fall so that a new system can come forward to stake its claim. These statements are borne out in the testimony of the participants who were interviewed in the data collection phase of this study included later in chapters 4 and 5.

It is a lofty goal that all children will attain proficiency on state-mandated assessments, but is it realistic—or even possible? Is there any school district in the country where 100% of the students are passing these assessments? A passing rate of 100% is what President Bush mandated through NCLB. Think of what measures schools have gone through to try to reach this goal. As the 2014 mandate grew nearer educators realized that even though great efforts were made and vast amounts of money were spent, failure was still the final outcome. This is the result of the No Child Left Behind program: raise the standards and require unrealistic percentages of passing until all schools fail. Keep in mind, when the term *passing percentages* is used, it is referring to subgroups' passing percentages, not individual student passing percentages. This fact is lost on many individuals outside the education profession. The passing percentage for a student to pass the test may be set at 65% or 70%, but the subgroup percentage rises much higher, keeping in line with AYP percentages. When subgroup-passing percentages rose to 83% in 2011, mass failure of schools and school districts began to occur across the country. This is central to understanding the grounded theory presented for this study. When all schools see failure as the inevitable outcome and the stakes are too high to allow failure to occur, then the states will accept the offer to escape the penalties. Along with the escape offer come the necessary changes to school programs to bring them under total federal control. The states will comply and capitulate to the subjugation. After all, they must follow the law. This is why AYP was put into law.

Hegelian Dialectic

The complete subjugation of public education is being carried out to its natural, planned conclusions through use of a form of deceptive coercion that all governments use to carry out the manipulation of their populace. This is the use of what is called *the dialectic*, referring to the Hegelian dialectic. It is a planned assault on the emotions and the intellect of hardworking men and women down through the ages. It is still used today with expert finesse. The dialectic is simple. Thesis, antithesis, synthesis is the prescription for operation. Or to put this dialectic another way: problem, reaction, and solution. The problem is created, manipulated, and propagated. When the natural reaction comes from the people who are the oppressed and feel persecuted, the same forces step in to manage the reaction. Finally the solution is provided. The frustrated people accept the solution with thankful hearts. The people do not realize that it is all managed through the same entity that brought the crisis in the first place. The solution was predetermined. Each phase of the dialectic was planned.

The dialectic is difficult to understand until one sees it in practice. As previously mentioned, the dialectic is named for Georg Hegel, an 18th-century philosopher who saw his theory as a spiritual evolutionary process where with every synthesis came greater evolvement toward perfection. Its use, though, by the political and social planners through the ages is nothing short of diabolical. The dialectic has been used by many of the governments of the world for hundreds of years in the attempt to move the populace in a certain direction. It has been used by democracies as well as by totalitarian regimes. Marx and Engels, who lived in the nineteenth century, used it to perfection to set up their Communist world thought.

> Hegel's dialectic is the tool, which manipulates us into a frenzied circular pattern of thought and action. Every time we fight for or defend against an ideology we are playing a necessary role in Marx and Engels' grand design to advance humanity into a dictatorship of the proletariat. The synthetic Hegelian solution to all these conflicts can't be introduced unless we all take a side that will advance the agenda. (Raapana & Friedrich, 2005, para. 3)

Western capitalist governments have also used the dialectic. The dialectic is playing out in perfect harmony with the education agenda. We see the dialectic at work in many socialist programs created in the last 50 years, and it is hard not to argue that the dialectic is being played to perfection when it comes to education. Thinking logically, the system has been broken by design. When the 100% proficiency mandate was given to Congress in 2002 by President Bush, every congressman and congresswoman stood up and cheered, not realizing they were playing right into the hands of the dialectic.

In Hegelian dialectic fashion, the problem was self-evident, but it had taken many years to reach this point when President Bush made his declaration. The schools across America were in trouble and were that way for many reasons. Society had broken down and become destabilized. The family saw huge changes since the days when mothers stayed at home and had the energy to raise their children and help them with their homework. Large high schools that had been operating effectively with only one assistant principal now needed seven to ten just to keep up with the discipline referrals from the teachers. More and more students were graduating but could not seem to function in college without remediation classes. Faith in the education system was abysmal in polls taken across the country. The Gallup Poll in 2012 found (Burke, 2012) that only 29% of the American public had confidence in the public school system. The public demanded accountability. This cry, or reaction, from the public helped to usher in the standardized test as the pathway that would measure accountability. With President Bush's federal NCLB policies and penalties for AYP non-compliance, the education system was taken to the breaking point. The solution was now ready for its unveiling. Exactly what form the new system will look like is not clear at this time. One thing is for sure, however: the dictates will come from the federal level and all states will comply. As it appears now, the public school system will be a combination of traditional public schools and public charter schools. With the amount of money that is flowing into charter schools, it is likely this method of schooling will play a major role in the education of students in the future.

Overcoming Cognitive Dissonance

As discussed previously, the other powerful force working in the minds of people who accept the current system built around the overuse of testing is *cognitive dissonance.*

> Cognitive dissonance occurs when people are faced with thought patterns that disturb their mental equilibrium, and they seek balance in their thinking in order to escape a paradigm of thinking that makes them uncomfortable. They need a state of normalcy that makes them feel in sync with the forces that guide the political, religious, social, and economic engines of the world. The person who feels uncomfortable will find ways to bring the normalcy pattern back into balance with systems of thought that may or may not be rooted in reality. (Cherry, 2012)

In the education system of today, administrators, teachers, parents, and students are looking for balance and seeking some sense of normalcy. Schools that are reported as failing have to be viewed in reality, not by a standard that in any other system would be seen as unjust. Are they really failing, or is the standard of measurement a tool for the government to use to produce a result that promotes an agenda for a predetermined outcome? As long as people do not confront the issues and step out of this false picture of normalcy, the system will continue. As the status quo continues, knowledge is limited and learning stifled.

This study focused on school communities in two locations. The first was the east-side community Austin, where the schools have operated the same for generations. The second was the North Forest community on the north side of Houston, where they lost their entire school district. The state education agency closed the district due to low performance issues that occurred for years—low performance as measured by the accountability system and AYP-mandated standards. Poverty was an issue, as was generational welfare. The communities in both locations were proud and family ties were strong. Until recently, students were able to matriculate through the system and work toward their diplomas. Many students received good educations and translated that into college or into a vocational profession. Yes, some students dropped out and went to work. This is always going to be the case in a free society. Students have the option and freedom to drop out of school if they choose. Even though states have laws against students dropping out of school, many choose to do so anyway. School officials should always work to prevent this and encourage students to complete their education. Teachers should always work to educate their students to the best of their ability and inspire them with quality instruction. It is not, however, always going to happen that all students make it to graduation day. With NCLB, though, all students have to make it to graduation day or the school is penalized. Sanctions are taken against those schools that don't measure up, and eventually some schools, especially from high poverty areas, eventually are restructured due to the dictates of the law according to NCLB. When the restructuring occurs, there are many manufacturers that stand ready to supply the needed instructional tools that the newly created charter school needs for its operation.

Consider the argument against restructuring of all schools that fail to achieve AYP compliance, but especially high schools. High school students make up the largest category affected by AYP mandates. Yet when a high school is restructured, the students are partitioned off to other high schools in the area. Only a small percentage of the existing students are allowed to attend the charter school, either through selection or lottery. What about the majority of the students that are in need of remediation? Are their needs addressed at the new school they now attend? How do their deficiencies affect the new school's AYP rating they are now attending? Would not money devoted to the new charter school be better served by keeping all of the students at the school that has failed and working to address the students' deficiencies? Instead, the system moves schools to failure with high AYP-mandated percentages, and then punishes the school for not successfully raising enough students to proficiency. The notion that all students will be proficient is totally unrealistic. To expect schools to meet the 85%, and especially the 2013 mandate of 92.5% (taking an average of the ELA and Math requirements), proficiency requirement is expecting the highly improbable. This mandate is not rooted in reality. Many variables in society will always affect student failures in public education. Most of these variables are beyond the control of the individual school serving the community. Yet *failing schools* continue to be sanctioned.

Maybe this mandate could be applied to a private school by an individual school board using a very small student population, but certainly not to a public school. It especially cannot apply to every large or small, urban or suburban, city or country, public school in the entire nation. It is for this reason that the 100% proficiency mandate for 2014 should be reviewed, with the option to consider a more realistic approach in the education of all children. The NCLB 100% mandate has the most effect on the very schools the system should be trying to improve: low-performing, high-minority schools in urban settings of poverty.

Compounding the difficulties the schools face each year is the issue of underfunding by the federal government. The mandates are in place, yet the funding is grossly inadequate. The 2009 presidential budget appropriations related to No Child Left Behind (Lee, 2009) had a funding gap that was reported by the National Education Association (NEA). The gap amounted to $80 billion between what was needed to keep pace with inflation and the budget request made by President Bush for 2009 projections. This also applied to funding for Title I grants from the 2008 allotments. In this case (Lee, 2009) there was a $50 billion shortfall. This shortfall of funds affected the state education agencies that distribute funds to local school districts. When the federal government withholds necessary funds from the states to operate the mandated programs, the result is that the states withhold funds from the local school districts. Withholding funds forces the local school districts to make cuts in their budget in order to fund the programs that are mandated by the federal government. The proper funding issue goes to the heart of the intent of NCLB from its onset in 2002. The extreme measures of punishment for failure to meet AYP, coupled with the failure of the federal government to at least supply the necessary appropriations to give schools a fighting chance to meet AYP, are problematic at best.

Understanding the Grounded Theory

The grounded theory that was tested in this study was the following: NCLB is a policy that intentionally moves schools, especially those in urban settings, to failure, with the intended outcome of forcing schools to adopt a new education curriculum for new outcomes. The theory came out of research embedded in the literature written on the mandates and policies of NCLB. The theory was also formulated from my experience in the field as a teacher, an assistant principal, and a principal who observed and was a part of the intense high-stakes testing format. Beginning with TABS, then TEAMS, followed by TAAS, then TAKS, and finally STAAR, the students of Texas (and all other states using their own testing programs) have been tested for 30 years, only to see their scores continually fall when compared with other students in international comparisons. AYP mandates have driven schools further away from the goal of NCLB to require all students to be proficient on the test. The intense pressure of high-stakes testing has extracted a toll on the education profession that is immeasurable. The damage to the children, who have had their psyches threatened with failure year after year, has had incalculable consequences. Based on the research, an analysis of NCLB law, and inductive reasoning and logic, this researcher concluded that NCLB was, from its conception in the minds of its planners, designed to drive schools to failure so that a new system could be established that would support an entirely different approach to educating the youth of America.

Summation

"In politics, nothing happens by accident. If it happens, you can bet it was planned that way" (Allen, 1972, p. 8). This quote, often attributed to Franklin D. Roosevelt, president of the United States during the Great Depression and most of World War II, demonstrates the careful arrangement of events in government and politics. In light of the information brought to light, can it be concluded that the events of the last 50 years have been a coincidence? Or have they been a well orchestrated, unfolding chain of events that led to opportunistic, wealthy philanthropists and software billionaires rushing to the rescue to save what was left of a school system that was broken and, more important, broken by design? Has our government, one administration working seamlessly into the next administration, been a willing contributor allowing these events to take place? Examining the information presented and taking into account the seamless progression toward school failure from one federal governmental administration to the next, one is led to question the impact of the mechanism used that led to the breakdown of the school system. The subsequent implementations of accountability standards and school failures have contributed to the erosion of the public education system, resulting in its eventual subjugation.

One must wonder where the education system in America is headed. Perhaps a public/private partnership where the corporate system is the model, and the only thing that counts is the product. The quality of the outcome as seen in the product is correlated to the quality of the outcome on the test produced by the child. Success on the yearly assessment translates to a successful company/school. The public, as well as those who work in the public school systems across America, need to ask themselves this question: is the public school system worth saving? Consider the two paradigms that exist in today's education community as stated by Dr. Ravitch.

The response to the current crisis in education tends to reflect two different worldviews. On one side are those who call themselves "reformers." The reformers believe that the schools can be improved by more testing, more punishment of educators (also known as "accountability"), more charter schools, and strict adherence to free-market principles in relation to employees (teachers) and consumers (students). On the other are those who reject the reformers' proposals and emphasize the importance of addressing the social conditions—especially poverty—that are the root causes of poor academic achievement. Many of these people— often parents in the public school system, experienced teachers, and scholars of education—favor changes based on improving curriculum, facilities, and materials, improving teacher recruitment and preparation, and attending to the cognitive, social, and emotional development of children. The critics of test-based accountability and free-market policies do not have a name, so the reformers call them "anti-reform." It might be better to describe them as defenders of common sense and sound education. (Ravitch, 2011, para. 11)

What will it take to make the necessary corrective measures to put our public school systems back where they belong? It is only through a well-educated, highly informed populace that a democratic society can operate effectively. Important decisions lie ahead for all who seek the profession of teaching and wish to influence the minds of children for the future. Equally important decisions lie ahead for superintendents and the leadership of school districts. Will they fight for their teachers and their school districts, or sink into a system of commonality where knowledge and information are administered through the computer and achievement is measured solely by a common test? Will states capitulate to the federal government and accept a new curriculum standard that brings all school districts in the nation under one federal system? Will charter schools and vouchers become the prevailing avenue for parents in their decisions of where to place their child for his or her education? The education profession is at a crossroad. There is no time to waste. In the next two chapters the data from the research are revealed. This data that was obtained through personal interviews with those who experienced the endgame of No Child Left Behind proves very revealing.

Chapter 4

Research Conducted in Pursuit of the Grounded Theory

The purpose of the study, research questions, methodology involved in the research, and collections of data are all reviewed in chapter 4. Qualitative data were described and analyzed from multiple interviews with those affected directly by No Child Left Behind mandates. The consequences of not meeting standards set forth in No Child Left Behind mandates resulted in restructure or closure of the schools in the study. The failure to meet standards impacted the lives of students, parents, and all the education professionals involved in the groups studied. In this chapter data collected from the participants were taken from my dissertation and presented as they were obtained either through personal one-on-one interviews or through phone interviews. Much of the methodology to obtain the conclusions was left intact from my dissertation, so that it would be clear as to how the information was obtained and how the process and the protocols were applied.

As stated previously, but repeated for clarity: The purpose of this study, which was conducted as a qualitative grounded theory dissertation, was twofold. The first purpose was to present a grounded theory that described the perceptions of the parents, teachers, and administrators located in two geographical locations. Each group shared a common denominator of school failure due to AYP non-compliance. One group was located in the diverse community located on the east side of Austin, Texas. The other group was located on the north side of Houston, Texas. The study highlighted the perceptions of the parents and educators impacted by the restructuring of the neighborhood schools and their perceptions of the No Child Left Behind (NCLB) policies that affected their families, their profession, and the communities. The second purpose of the study was to bring awareness to the beneficiaries of NCLB mandates that drive education policies. The study sought to determine who benefits from the federal AYP and the state accountability system and who the victims are. From the research in the literature and the dual purpose of the study, a theory was presented that sought to explain the intent of NCLB and demonstrate its impact on parents and the education profession. Clarity and understanding unfolded through this study that will serve to aid parents and education professionals and, hopefully, bring changes in education policy.

Research Questions for Investigation

Laws written by the state and federal governments govern school operations and the education profession. School officials are charged with adhering to the laws that govern the operations of schools. There is no leeway for avoiding the law. I sought answers to the following important questions to guide the research study.

1. From the evidence presented, have the NCLB mandates served to propel schools and school districts toward AYP non-compliance?
2. What are the perceptions of parents toward the restructuring or closure of their neighborhood schools?
3. What are the perceptions of teachers and administrators who have been involved in the restructuring or school closure process?
4. What are the perceptions of parents of children affected through the restructuring of the neighborhood schools with regard to their representation in their taxation?

The remainder of chapter 4 is designed to explain data provided through interviews conducted in the two regions in Texas. After data are analyzed and explained, a summary is provided. In this section the participants revealed their struggle to deal with the aftermath of decisions made by their school districts and the guiding authorities of the State of Texas after No Child Left Behind mandates were not achieved over at least a five-year period of time, resulting in failure and intervention. Very important to keep in mind in both of these locations is that failure was defined only through the eyes of NCLB mandates. The percentages required in the subgroups, as explained earlier, were too high and unrealistic for schools facing multiple challenges revolving around low-income or poverty conditions in the school communities.

In both locations parents were interviewed. In the Houston group, teachers and administrators were interviewed as well as parents. The one thing both parent groups had in common was their children's education being disrupted through a declaration of failure due to continued inability to achieve Adequate Yearly Progress (AYP). For the Austin group, which was a section of Austin ISD, the penalty for continued noncompliance was the planned restructure of the vertical team of schools feeding into the high school. For the north Houston group that went by the name the North Forest ISD, the penalty was the loss of sovereignty of the entire school district. Every school in the district was closed, every professional employee lost his or her job, and the board of trustees that represented the people was disbanded. All of this was legal according to No Child Left Behind law.

The professional educators interviewed from the North Forest ISD provided a perspective on the effects of No Child Left Behind mandates that the parents could not provide. This information proved extremely valuable. The work-related pressures educators felt were revealed when their efforts did not produce the needed results, despite hours of extra effort with the students. The pressures were a result of involvement in the School Improvement Program dictated to schools that are not meeting Adequate Yearly Progress in their subgroup percentages of passing the state test that is given yearly. It should be noted the data presented were not meant to compare or contrast the results of the data in the groups interviewed. The data are presented to reflect the support, or lack of support, for the research questions presented in the study. The reason education professionals were not interviewed from the Austin ISD is that this researcher was denied access to the schools. The reason for denial of access was that the district administration did not want the teachers and administration distracted any further. The east side schools of the Austin ISD have been the subject of much talk and speculations amongst the media and the public, about the success or failure taking place in the schools. The school district administration felt the challenges the teachers and administration faced were too great for the schools to undergo any further distractions. Having been a principal and being aware of the high stakes involved in testing outcomes, I understood this decision and was resigned to the fact that I did not need to press any further to attempt to get a different decision.

Since the time of the initial writing of this dissertation, the Austin parents on the east side had significant changes made in the status of the school developments. Through the efforts of an organized resistance within the east side community, pressure was brought to bear on the school board and the superintendent that resulted in the charter management organization being removed as an educational change agent in the schools targeted for restructuring. Accomplished also by the parents was the successful placement of three new school board members that pledged to represent their interest in their neighborhood schools. When the CMO was removed from the district after one school year of operation, the school district had a unique problem. The CMO had already started operations in one elementary school, with plans to implement the same program in a middle school and high school. Now decisions had to be made for the future purpose of the elementary school. It remained closed for the 2013–2014 school year.

Austin ISD has an open enrollment policy. The parents who rejected the charter school relocated to other elementary schools in the area that could accommodate the added enrollment. The school most affected by the restructuring policy was Allan Elementary. Allan Elementary was not a school in danger of failing AYP. They had an acceptable rating by the Texas Education Agency. They were only chosen for restructure because the CMO that was hired to try to improve learning outcomes wanted a vertical alignment of schools feeding into Eastside Memorial High School. The CMO wanted all the vertical team of schools under their charter management operation. The parents had made clear their voice against any charter school takeover. They had made this perfectly clear with the Austin Board of Trustees and the officials of Austin ISD.

Due to the open enrollment policy, a significant number of parents opted out of having their children attend the new charter school that was Allan Elementary.

Allan Elementary is no longer operating as an elementary school. It has now been turned into a professional development center for the teachers of Austin ISD. For Eastside Memorial High School, a company that specializes in working with teachers to raise student test scores, was hired to work only with the high school to raise its accountability standards to an acceptable rating. The Texas Education Agency gave the school district two years to allow this company to produce positive results or face closure of the high school. Had it not been for the activism of the parents many more students would have been affected by the encroachment of the charter management company. Now the focus is only on the high school; where it should have been all along. At the time of this writing, a new development took place with the resignation of the Austin ISD superintendent. The superintendent who oversaw the restructuring measures moved to another large metropolitan school district in the southeast region of the country.

The other location selected for data collection was located in the southeast section of the State of Texas within the city limits of Houston but not a part of Houston ISD and was in an urban setting that struggles with low-income social conditions typical of many urban centers in the country. This was the North Forest ISD. Due to continued AYP failure, and some questionable leadership, it was set apart by the State of Texas who shut down the entire school district. The school district's board of trustees was disbanded, and every employee had his or her contract dissolved. Each employee was left to find employment in another school district. The parents in the school district lost their representation, leaving them without a voice and local support through an elected school board representative.

The following represents the opinions, perceptions, and attitudes of those interviewed who were affected by the decisions of school district and state officials. Each decision made by state authorities was made within the guidelines set forth through the No Child Left Behind mandates. To review information provided in chapter 2, five options (U.S. Department of Education, n.d. a) are available to a district when one of its Title I schools has five consecutive years of AYP failure in the same category; the options are as follows:

1. Reopen the school as a public charter school.
2. Replace all or most of school staff, including the principal.
3. Enter into a contract with an entity, such as a private management company, with a demonstrated record of effectiveness to operate the school.
4. Have the state take over the school.
5. Impose another major restructuring of the school's governance arrangement (Texas Education Agency, 2012).

Data Collection

As previously stated, two communities in Texas were chosen for the sampling populations for this study. One was chosen from the east side of Austin in the Austin ISD. For the purpose of identification from this point forward in the dissertation, the name for this sampling population is Group 1. This community is a very diverse section of the city, with a sizable portion comprising Hispanic heritage. Using the high school in the community and taking data from the last obtainable Academic Excellence Indicator System (AEIS) report from 2012 (Texas Education Agency, AEIS Report, 2012), ethnic breakdown indicates 80% of the population is Hispanic, with African Americans comprising 16.1% of the population.

The second community chosen for the sampling population is an urban community located just north of Houston, Texas, in the formerly North Forest ISD. The name of this sampling population is Group 2. Using the AEIS report from 2012 for the representative high school in the community (Texas Education Agency, AEIS Report, 2012), African Americans comprise 66% of the population, with Hispanics comprising 30.9% of the population.

One very important statistic that both communities share is an extremely large percentage of the population falling in the Economically Disadvantaged category, according to the AEIS report (Texas Education Agency, AEIS Report, 2012). For the east-side community in Austin (Group

1), 91.3% of the population is categorized as Economically Disadvantaged. In the urban center located just north of Houston in what was the former North Forest ISD (Group 2), 100% of the population is categorized as Economically Disadvantaged (2012). Both communities' high schools were in the School Improvement Program, mandated through the federal Department of Education for any school that has failed to meet standards with AYP for two or more years in a row. Both high schools had reached the point of restructuring, mandated from five or more years failing to meet standards with AYP.

Data were collected for both groups, first through surveys and, after the surveys, interviews. One problem this researcher faced in sending out the initial surveys was the unavailability of computers in the homes of the participants that were sought. With this in mind, those who did provide survey information and agreed to sit for an interview gave other names of people they thought would be interested in providing information for the study. This produced the snowball or chain form of sampling strategies this researcher planned to use, as stated below in the Types of Sampling section.

Types of Sampling

I made available two types of sampling, defined by Creswell (2007) as snowball or chain and criterion sampling. Creswell defines snowball or chain sampling as "cases of interest from people who know people who know what cases are information-rich" (p. 127). Criterion sampling is defined by Creswell (2007) as "cases that meet some criterion; useful for quality assurance" (p. 127).

Another issue this researcher faced involved the original intent to interview education professionals from both groups. In the case of Group 1, I was denied access to the schools by the External Research Department of Austin ISD. The reason given was that my access would be too disruptive to the teaching environment of the school and there was too much at stake to allow a disruption to occur. I understood the magnitude of their problem and accepted this denial of access without an appeal. To restate the magnitude of their problem: the high school was facing closure, and the administration and the teachers needed all their attention focused on meeting standards. Since I was a former high school principal, I understood the problem. This effectively eliminated this important group from taking part in the study. Parents of Group 1, however, still took part in the study and provided valuable information and perspectives. In the process of attending meetings related to the restructuring of the Austin schools, I met one individual who gave me tremendous insight into what was occurring in the schools and the community. This individual was a parent of children who attended Allan Elementary. This parent's willingness to confide in this researcher aided greatly in finding other parents willing to talk and share their stories.

In the case of Group 2, parents and educational professionals participated in the study, providing a full perspective on the issues addressed. The only issue faced with Group 2 was the workplace location for the education professionals and the needed names and phone numbers for the parents. To restate the situation, all the education professionals of Group 2 were fired. They now worked in different buildings all over the Houston area. One valuable contact was made with an education professional that was formerly employed in North Forest ISD. This individual provided extremely important information about the history of what happened in North Forest. He also provided other contacts involving parents and education professionals who were willing to let their stories be told. From the initial information from this valuable and important individual, other contacts were made, and the snowball effect provided additional contact names, phone numbers, and workplace locations. Since the school district where the education professionals were employed no longer existed and none of the professional contacts worked in the school district that absorbed the schools, no permission was needed to interview the education professionals.

Data collection began with survey distribution in January 2014. Interviews were conducted from February through May 2014. Interviews were recorded and converted to a digital program used for transcription by this researcher. Transcribed interviews were then converted to the NVivo-10 software program, where data were analyzed. This researcher analyzed the data in search of themes that would support or not support the research questions.

Selection of Participants

Participants for interviews were selected through a purposeful selection process. The original intent was to use a random purposeful sampling, but when the selection pool became limited due to very few surveys returned to the researcher, a different approach was taken. The selection of the participants moved more to purposeful sampling using the snowball or chain type of sampling, as well as the criterion type of sampling. Creswell (2007) stated that criterion sampling is favorable when the participants have all experienced the same phenomenon. Creswell goes on to state, "in a grounded theory study, the researcher chooses participants who can contribute to the development of the theory" (2007, p. 128).

Scheduling Interviews

Participants selected for interviews were contacted either by e-mail or directly by phone. Once agreement was made for the time, date, and location, the interview was placed on the calendar. Participants were eager to be included in the study and anxious to tell their stories.

Demographics and Background Information of Participants

Participant 1. Participant 1 was a 71-year-old African American male. He was the last principal of one of the high schools in Group 2. After he was removed from his post, the school district consolidated the two high schools into one and renamed the one remaining high school. This participant spent 40 years in the profession. He holds a master's degree in education. He is currently retired.

Participant 2. Participant 2 is an African American male 55 years in age. He worked as an assistant principal at the newly created high school in Group 2. When the school district identified as Group 2 was dissolved by the Texas Education Agency, this participant lost his job. He found work as an assistant principal in a neighboring school district. He has served eight years in the profession and holds a PhD.

Participant 3. Participant 3 is a 62-year-old African American female. She was a vocational teacher at the high school represented in Group 2, teaching cosmetology. She lost her position as the cosmetology teacher when the district dissolved and found the same job at a neighboring school district. She is currently in her 22nd year in the profession and holds a bachelor's degree.

Participant 4. Participant 4 is a 35-year-old African American female. She lost her job as a communications applications teacher at the high school represented in Group 2 when the school district was dissolved. She was able to find the same teaching assignment at a high school in a neighboring school district. She is in her 15th year of teaching and holds a master's degree in education.

Participant 5. Participant 5 is a 62-year-old African American female single mother. She worked as a volunteer in the school district while her children were in the schools represented in Group 2. She volunteered for 12 years in various schools. She was a community organizer and was active in helping to disseminate information and confront local school officials and politicians. She holds a degree from the local community college.

Participant 6. Participant 6 is a 56-year-old African American female who volunteered in the Group 2 school system while her two sons went through the schools in that district. She was instrumental in working for change and improvements in the schools represented in Group 2. She has a degree from a community college.

Participant 7. Participant 7 is a 34-year-old Hispanic male. He and his wife are the parents of two children attending one of the schools represented in Group 1. They both became active in their children's school and the school district and worked to hold the school district accountable for the restructuring of the school their children attended. He holds a bachelor's degree.

Participant 8. Participant 8 is a 48-year-old White female representing Group 1. She is a parent who helped to organize other parents who wanted to become active in the community and in the decisions of the school district that affect their children. Her two boys are now grown, with one out of school and one a senior in high school. She holds a degree from the community college.

Participant 9. Participant 9 is a 35-year-old White male. He and his wife have two daughters who are currently in an elementary school represented in Group 1. Their daughters did not attend one of the restructured schools, but they were in the vertical team of the high school represented in Group 1. He became active in the organization working for changes and improvements with the school district. He was a computer software developer and holds a bachelor's degree.

Participant 10. Participant 10 is a 66-year-old White male who was a structural engineer by profession. He was associated with Group 1 through his work as a project consultant in conflict resolution. His expertise in this field and his friendship with a former superintendent and Texas school commissioner brought him into dialogue with the parents of Group 1. He worked to bridge the gap that existed between certain groups and the district administration represented in Group 1.

Participant 11. Participant 11 is a 61-year-old African American female. She worked in the counseling office as a counselor's assistant at the high school represented in Group 2. One of her many tasks was to help students applying for college scholarships. Through this she was able to gain access to many students' records and observe firsthand the excellent work the students were accomplishing. She also observed firsthand the various groups that were coming into the district from the outside in an attempt to help teachers who were looking for ways to improve the state test scores.

Participant 12. Participant 12 is a 90-year-old African American male who was a former principal and school board member with 60 years of experience in the education profession. He spent much of his career in the school district represented by Group 2. He brought a perspective to the data that is broad and all encompassing. He knows the past, and he understands what happened to cause the school district to fall on hard times. It was an honor for this researcher to sit down with him for an interview.

Participant 13. Participant 13 is a former student at the high school represented in Group 2. He went on to receive his bachelor's degree from Louisiana State University and furthered his education, receiving a master's degree from Columbia University in New York City. He is currently in the doctoral program at Columbia University. He is an excellent representative for his former school and demonstrates that you cannot judge a school or a school district by the results on a standardized test. His future plan, once his doctoral studies are complete, is to hopefully teach at Rice University.

I am tremendously grateful for the individuals who agreed to share their experience with me. They certainly did not need to take time out of their day to allow me to intrude into their world. Each of these individuals, however, saw elements of where I was going with this information. Each of them cares deeply about the children and the schools in their communities. They know the value of a good education, and they can detect when they are being taken advantage of and treated in a manner that does not respect their culture or their heritage. The officials in their school districts and at the state level severely underestimated their resolve and determination.

There are two individuals represented in the participants that I could not have accomplished this data collection without their assistance. One individual in Group 1 and one individual in Group 2 saw my vision for this study and agreed to share their expert testimony and provide names of other people they felt would offer valuable advice and knowledge about the events that transpired in their communities. The information contained in chapters 4 and 5 could not have been collected without their help. Their willingness to assist in this study demonstrated the degree of commitment they had to their cause of fighting the power base that was so greatly affecting their lives.

Table 2

Participant Demographic Data

Participant	Parent or ed. professional	Job or position	Education level	Gender	Ethnicity	Age
1	Ed. professional	Principal (retired)	Masters	Male	African American	71
2	Ed. professional	Asst. principal	PhD.	Male	African American	55
3	Ed. professional	Teacher	Bachelors	Female	African American	62
4	Ed. professional	Teacher	Masters	Female	African American	35

5	Parent	Retired	Junior college	Female	African American	62
6	Parent	Retired	Junior college	Female	African American	56
7	Parent	Business	Bachelors	Male	Hispanic	34
8	Parent	Business	Junior college	Female	White	48
9	Parent	Business	Bachelors	Male	White	35
10	Ed. prof. consultant	Business	Masters	Male	White	66
11	Ed. para-professional	Counselor office	Junior college	Female	African American	61
12	School board member (ret)	Principal (retired)	Masters	Male	African American	90
13	Former student	Grad. asst.	Masters	Male	African American	24

Factors Affecting AYP for Group 1 and Group 2

In order to gain a representation of data for comparisons with the community of both groups, the high school that represents each community was used to demonstrate Adequate Yearly Progress outcomes. These outcomes are displayed in Tables 3, 4, and 5. Table 3 illustrates factors affecting AYP for Group 1 and Group 2 in 2012.

Table 3

Factors Affecting AYP for Group 1 and Group 2 in 2012 (TEA, AEIS Report, 2012)

Group	Percentage that met standard on state test	Attendance rate	Graduation rate	Percentage eco-disadvantage
1	78%	85.8	58.9%	* 91.3%
2	66%	88.6	59.2%	* 100%

*Of special note is the high percentage of economically disadvantaged students represented in both groups.

In 2012, the percentage of each subgroup that took the state test was required to reach a percentage of at least 87% in Reading/English Language Arts and 83% in Math. Tables 4 and 5 indicate the percentages reached by each of the subgroups' testing population; Table 4 represents Group 1, and Table 5 represents Group 2. This information was pulled from the 2012 AEIS report developed for each public school in the State of Texas. The data is taken from the high school of each group in the eleventh grade to demonstrate the numbers and the difficulties each group had in meeting standards. These percentages were not a representation of each school in the group studied, but they indicated the difficulty each group was having mastering the test. The subgroups represent the federal AYP groupings applied to all schools. (Note: As of the 2013-2014 school year, subgroups in Texas expanded to include 10 groupings.)

Table 4

Subgroups' Percentage of Met Standards for Reading/ELA and Math Group 1 (TEA, AEIS Report, 2012)

	African American	Hispanic	White	Economic disadvantaged	ELL	Special education
Reading/ ELA	90%	67%	*	71%	27%	50%
Math	57%	75%	*	70%	42%	55%

- Population percentage not high enough (10%) to count.
- ELL refers to English Language Learners

Table 5

Subgroups' Percentage of Met Standards for Reading/ELA and Math Group 2 (TEA AEIS Report, 2012)

	African American	Hispanic	White	Economic disadvantaged	ELL	Special education
Reading/ ELA	77%	89%	*	80%	*	35%
Math	81%	77%	*	80%	*	38%

* Population percentage not high enough (10%) to count.

Tables 4 and 5 illustrate the enormous difficulty urban schools located in sections of the city with high percentages of people in low-income or poverty brackets have with standardized tests and the unrealistic expectations mandated through No Child Left Behind AYP requirements. This situation has existed for years, and certainly in the entire era of No Child Left Behind. The system has not resulted in the needed improvements in accountability the US Department of Education espoused, and yet the governmental structures continue to apply the punitive sanctions against the schools and districts as if the results will be different.

Qualitative Analysis of Data

In order to gain dependable, credible, and trustworthy analysis of the data from the interviews, this researcher purchased and utilized the QSR International's NVivo 10 computer software. "NVivo helps manage, shape, and analyze qualitative data" (Creswell, 2007, p. 167). NVivo allows the researcher to find meaningful passages from the transcribed interviews that are placed in categories called *nodes*. From the nodes, the emerging themes become evident. For the purpose of this dissertation, the researcher used a query to develop a matrix that clearly indicated where emerging themes intersected with the research questions.

The intersections in the data are illustrated in Table 6. To review, the research questions are as follows:

1. From the evidence presented, have the NCLB mandates served to propel schools and school districts toward AYP noncompliance?
2. What are the perceptions of parents toward the restructuring or closure of their neighborhood schools?
3. What are the perceptions of teachers and administrators who have been involved in the restructuring or school closure process?
4. What are the perceptions of parents of children affected through the restructuring of the neighborhood schools with regard to their representation in their taxation?

Emerging Themes

Using NVivo 10 software, this researcher performed word frequency queries along with related information from topics brought forth and covered in the literature review, to establish emerging themes from the interviews. This researcher developed a matrix using the NVivo 10 program and was able to see those intersections of emerging themes by applying responses to the research questions and correlating relevancy to the grounded theory presented in the dissertation. Each number represents the number of times the emerging theme correlated to a research question.

Table 6

Matrix Query of Emerging Themes

	AYP	Business interest	Charter schools	Society issues	Factors in test failure	Leadership failure	Instructional changes	Student issues
Q1	40	7	5	4	17	17	1	16
Q2	18	8	11	6	6	31	2	12
Q3	38	9	9	6	21	33	5	19
Q4	0	0	1	2	2	3	0	0

(Note to clarify: Business interests referred to corporate or local businesses that were interested in school failure in order to move a charter school into the community.

Instructional changes refer to the constant changes in curriculum due to new state tests, or new strategies to adopt to attempt to improve test scores.)

Participant Responses for Each Research Question and Emerging Themes

After reviewing the matrix query, this researcher extracted the dominant emerging themes categories for each research question and presented statements from the participants. The following are excerpts taken from the transcripts that reveal information correlating the emerging theme with the research questions. As the testimonies are read, it is important to keep in mind that each of their experiences was a direct result of No Child Left Behind policies and mandates. Instead of helping these families, No Child Left Behind served to punish the parents and their children only because their school could not keep up with the AYP percentages required in one or more subgroups.

Research question one. From the evidence presented, have the No Child Left Behind mandates served to propel schools and school districts toward AYP noncompliance?

Emerging theme one: Adequate Yearly Progress (AYP).

Several themes emerged from the participants in the NVivo 10 data analysis. The data collected indicated a dominant perception that No Child Left Behind did serve to propel schools and school districts to failure. The participants pointed out that the mechanism used to propel schools to failure was the Adequate Yearly Progress (AYP) mandate. As evidenced in the following testimony, if it had not been for the AYP percentage mandate elevating beyond reason, the schools would not have been labeled as failing.

Participant 1 (Group 2) said:

> One of the most glaring problems with No Child Left Behind is dictating mandates without the money provided to help accomplish the mandates. Then there is the mandate of 100% of the children passing the test. Really, that goal is unrealistic. Everybody can't pass. Society doesn't work that way. No Child Left Behind has not served all the kids' needs, mainly from the standpoint of a lack of resources. If all things are equal, yes, maybe all kids can pass, but that's not what is happening. Things are not equal. They never will be equal. When you look at that thing, accountability and AYP, the schools that are failing based on where they are located and who is running the school, many have failed before. Those schools are not going to be successful. They already know that. They also know that the schools in the outer suburbs are going to be successful. Resources have so much to do with it. The closer in to the city, the tougher it gets. The issues in the urban areas are huge. It's not that the kids can't learn. It's the societal conditions that play such a huge role. Some of the kids can overcome the issues, but the majority cannot. Add to that a test that they have to pass, and it is not going to be a priority. But where we really got into trouble with No Child Left Behind was with AYP. We could not keep up with the percentages needed to pass.

Participant 2 (Group 2) stated:

> One of the main things affecting the district dealt with No Child Left Behind dictating mandates that were unfunded by the federal government. All the ancillary issues that were needed to bring students up to the levels that were dictated by the policy were left to the local districts to acquire. This put a huge strain on the local budgets. And this year, 2013–2014, we are expected to be 100%. What the general public doesn't understand is that you can't compare business standards and school education standards. With business if you get a defective product, you can send it back. You can't do that with a child. You have to work with what you get. Have the accountability system in Texas and the federal AYP standards served to move schools to noncompliance and school failure? With the way the system is set up, I would agree with that statement. Because the percentages to meet standards is a moving target and continually rising, and the funding is not provided to achieve the expectations, the groups that needed the extra help could not get the help they needed. The gaps were too wide, and with percentages to meet standards going up each year, it became an insurmountable mountain to climb. Add to this the cultural and societal issues that exist in areas of poverty, with both parents working and not at home, and many of the kids having to work when they get out of school every day, and the problems mount. No Child Left Behind does not address those issues. All it is concerned with is a test score. Education should develop the mind and spirit to make it in life. If the powers that be really wanted those things to happen, the money would have been provided to allow the school to do its job. The fact that the funds were withheld points to the fact that the powers that be did not want No Child Left Behind to succeed. And putting a percentage requirement of 100% by 2014 only

confirms that they did not want it to succeed and schools were doomed to failure. The federal government made into law what outcome they wanted but failed to provide the necessary means to achieve the intended outcome. Also one has to recognize that when the system went from TAAS to TAKS, a much more difficult test was given to the students. This was the same time that AYP was introduced and the 2014 mandate was established. All of these factors contributed to the challenge placed upon schools and school districts and made the challenge of meeting standards impossible to achieve.

Participant 10 (Group 1) said:

> Mainly, they devalued the lives of young people … if they did not have a satisfactory test score, they lost value. This is what No Child Left Behind did to every child. It reduced them to a test score. Because the product now became the student. The standards had to be applied to the product. It devalued them … We are currently not solving problems in education. Benjamin Franklin said, "Tell me and I forget; teach me and I remember; involve me and I learn." We are teaching in the first example. We tell and we tell, and we tell some more. We have to get to the involvement stage.

Participant 4 (Group 2) stated:

> The standards, the system, the penalties have all served to move schools down a path that eventually causes the state to move in. The standards continued to go up. We would just get to a point where we were catching up, and the standards would go up. With our kids from where they came from, it was impossible to keep up … It is killing the inner-city schools. It is bringing about the demise of a whole culture of kids.

Participant 9 (Group 1) said:

> So really, I have not seen anything worthwhile done with the data. I am on the CIC (Campus Improvement Council) on my campus, and it appears to me that people don't really know how to use the data ... I think No Child Left Behind exists to systematically undermine public education. It appears that it is almost starving the education system. This framework exists to put schools in an impossible situation that will ultimately lead to failure in terms of the accountability.

Participant 3 (Group 2), stated:

> I really do feel like in a lot of ways, schools have been set up to fail. If you keep raising the bar and we are still working at a lower level, then just when we begin to see some daylight, the standards are raised again ... it is a moving target that the kids are very frustrated with.

Participant 8 (Group 1) said:

> The stakes for the schools have been too high. It has not had good effects. It has become another stick to beat up on public education. There are forces at work, it appears to me, that are trying to kill off public education as we know it.

Participant 7 (Group 1) stated:

> It was No Child Left Behind that eventually took us down. At first it looked like it would be a good thing. We are a Title I district. We stood to gain from No Child Left Behind—or so we thought.

Emerging theme two: Factors in test failure.

Another key emerging theme the participants brought forth that supports research question one concerned the prevailing reasons for test failure.

Participant 2 (Group 2) said:

> In No Child Left Behind, once you enter the School Improvement Program, you have to have two years of a sustained level of meeting the standards in order to get out of the School Improvement Program. That means you have to meet standards in each subgroup. With the leadership issues we had, it became very difficult. During the seven years I was an assistant principal at the high school, I had one principal for the first two years; then every year after that, I had a different principal. We never could get out of the School Improvement Program because the board of trustees would not leave the principal in place to gain any consistency.

Participant 10 (Group 1) stated:

> All the evidence is saying now that school systems, with all the testing and pressure surrounding the testing issue, are damaging kids' lives. The people at the top in the school district, as in probably all districts, are completely disconnected from the kids at the bottom.

Participant 4 (Group 2) said:

> I tend to cite as one of the main contributing factors that led to test failure was the environment that the school was located in. The cultural elements are so different from some of the suburban districts. The family dynamics that contribute to the child's life are very difficult. With both parents working and some in jail, the kid's life is very difficult.

Participant 12 (Group 2) stated:

> I think a lot of it (failure) was about testing. You cannot judge a student by one test. Maybe you can judge about 25% by a test, if that. But you certainly can't judge the whole child by a test. You can't judge the worth of a school by a test, much less the worth of a school district.
>
> Testing does not reveal everything there is about a child. Many things are not testable. I'm a country boy. My children are from the city. My children went to an urban high school. They had different experiences from those in the country, different backgrounds, different experiences. You can't give one type of test to everybody.

Participant 5 (Group 2) said:

> One of the main things I saw (as a result of leadership turnover) was the students' behavior. The children were getting more and more out of control. With the change in principals yearly and the movement to hire teachers from other areas in the country, this led to instability; and we saw it in the attitudes and behaviors of the children.

Participant 1 (Group 2) stated:

> Our efforts received an acceptable rating from TEA for two years in a row. I was then replaced, and the program we were doing was replaced and the rating fell. Since that time the school district disbanded one high school and consolidated it into the other high school. Since 2005–2006 the new consolidated high school has had nine principals. Every year brought in a new principal with a new method. When teacher shortages began to be a problem, the board made the decision to bring in teachers from the Teach for America program. These teachers had huge problems. They weren't trained

in proper teaching methodology to begin with, and second, they weren't from anywhere around here. It takes a lot more than subject matter knowledge to be a teacher. You have to be a people person. You have to have a basic understanding of the culture. Effective teaching understands the culture of the children you are trying to teach. The turnover of the staff year-in and year-out is what contributed the most to the breakdown in the district. The test scores plummeted.

Participant 3 (Group 2) said:

As soon as the test scores did not come up, the existing principal was out, and a new one was brought in. The issue I had with that was that they were bringing in people who had no knowledge of the community, the parents, or the students.

Participant 8 (Group 1) said:

Our school district was also hit hard by the shortfall in funds in 2011. We are considered a property-rich district even though 70% of our students are eco-disadvantaged. At our high school the reduction in force accounted for one in three personnel being laid off. This hit our campus very hard. By the end of October, we had lost four teachers. By December we had lost 10 teachers. In January 2012, the kids came back to a new principal and a third of the staff being replaced either by substitute teachers or newly hired teachers. The success was really jeopardized because the students felt like second-class citizens and not worthy of anything good from the school district.

Research question two. What are the perspectives of parents toward the restructuring or closure of their neighborhood schools?
Emerging theme one: Leadership issues.

Key participant testimony central to the issue related to parent perspective on the restructuring or closure issue involving his or her school or school district emerged from the data. A clear voice came forth that a lack of leadership was prevalent leading up to and during the restructuring and closure process.

Participant 5 (Group 2) said:

> In one day every person who worked in the district lost their job. They were out of work. Some still don't have work today. How do the people who did this sleep at night? They are not just hurting the adults; they are hurting the children. They want this land.

Participant 6 (Group 2) stated:

> A lot of it has to do with the land that the school is located on and the community around it. This property is valuable. They are not putting any money in this community for a reason. There is a plan, and the schools are a part of it. We know that plans are made way ahead of time and things go on behind the scenes we know nothing about. Then all of a sudden, we find out that our district is shut down.

Participant 4 (Group 2) added:

> In my opinion our district was a targeted school district. Other schools are like ours with even worse scores. They have not sanctioned them. Several teachers I know in the district that the commissioner gave our schools to, told me they could not figure out why TEA was doing what they were doing to us. I look at other high schools close by in that district, and their scores are horrible. They aren't closing those schools down. This was very political, I am convinced. If the state wants our students to have a better opportunity, you should have sent us to the school district just north and west of us. They are a

better district, with better learning opportunities for the kids. It is apparent that it is about the money. They want the property that is here. We know this area is going to be expanded in the roadways. This was a hostile takeover.

Participant 5 (Group 2) said:

We were on the right track academically. We just didn't have the money or other resources to get it done quick enough for the state. The first thing they did was come in and begin tearing down the buildings. They closed and demolished the career center for vocational education that was right across the street from the main campus.

Participant 9 (Group 1) stated:

As I said, the school district administration did not include us until it was a done deal and we became very vocal and began attending school board meetings. Now they really pay attention to us. This is mainly due to the fact that we were able to get three board members replaced. The new board members organized the platform to get the charter management company replaced. Now the school district brought in a new working partner from Johns Hopkins University to assist the high school with getting their test scores up. They have two years to get the scores up to the point of meeting standards. If they fail, the plan is to close the school. My fifth grader does well and does not struggle with the test. But last year when she was in the fourth grade was the first year that I became aware of how stressed-out she was about the test. She had it in her mind that if she did not do well on the test, she would not move on to the next grade. She was in tears about the testing environment in the testing area in the room. It was very regimented and intimidating. The way the test is administered causes her stress. I became more attuned to the testing and its effect on my daughter at this time. It is not clear to me that the testing is good for her and good for the school. I'm not sure what exactly is being accomplished.

Participant 10 (Group 1) stated:

Our city has made it all about the superintendent for decades. They are very much a top-down hierarchical-power school district. The operations are still very much rooted in the old days of segregation. Going back to segregation days, many of the issues with the minority populations are rooted in how they have been treated through the years. The testing atmosphere now has compounded the existing problems because of the mandates and the high stakes involved. The statutes say that the district must bring the community in and work with the community in meaningful ways to serve the needs of the students. This is what the campus improvement committees are all about. But that is only a beginning. I am working with the school district's attorney on how to effectively work within this framework. Giving them how-tos. Our city likes to play the blame game. "The students are bad." "The teachers are bad." I began to get involved when the talk of bringing in the charter management company, IDEA, started. I went to a school board meeting and watched one of the students from the high school get up and talk to the school board about what was important to him and his family and friends, and he got degraded and cast aside by the superintendent ... Right there in public, she dismissed him. Gave him no credit. Teachers and administrators have to respect students if they expect students to respect them. We have started this process now. Students and administrators sitting down and having dialogue. Much of this dialogue has to be with the school board. They have to listen. If the school board is not involved, then it is left to the administration, and they are not always listening and oftentimes don't want to listen, especially at the central office level. Mix in the high-stakes testing atmosphere, and the situation gets worse. Just as in 1965 when we were segregating, something needed to happen. Same thing with No Child Left Behind. But the direction it took became very destructive. Punish them, threaten them, and they will change. No! Even in the business world, that does not effect change. Care, honor, respect, communicate, have success together, fail together—so you can also solve problems together.

Emerging theme two: AYP.

AYP had intersections with the parents' view of the school restructuring when they related it to the reasons for the restructuring.

Participant 9 (Group 1) said:

It soon became apparent that IDEA was going to institute a program that we were not in favor of. The philosophy was not in keeping with what we were used to in our schools. The parents began to opt out. Many parents pulled their kids out and sent them to other elementary schools. We were able to do this since the school district had an open-enrollment policy ... Oh, yeah. Absolutely, No Child Left Behind has definitely affected their education. Especially with the teachers and how they teach their classes now ... Testing and accountability is pervasive. It is always there in every conversation with a teacher.

Emerging theme three: Student issues.

Student issues, while having fewer intersections with research question two, are still worthy of mentioning due to the morale of the students. Students endured the scrutiny from the state over their capability revolving around their test scores and the threat of losing their school.

Participant 6 (Group 2) said:

> The constant change had a lot to do with the morale of the kids. They did not have any connection with the school after a while. The identity was lost; that added to them not wanting to come to school. Some of the programs were either cut or scaled back so much that the kids lost interest. Add to this a dysfunctional family, and the problems got compounded. The principal would take funds from the band program to pay for more instructional items, and pretty soon you didn't have a reason to enjoy school, and they soon lost interest.

Participant 4 (Group 2) stated:

> The family dynamics that contribute to the child's life are very difficult. With both parents working and some in jail, the kid's life is very difficult. Until you can get some type of normalcy in the student's life, it's hard to focus on school. In the early 2000s, TEA came to a faculty meeting, and this man had the nerve to say, after we explained the difficult situations in the community, he said, "We are concerned with the test scores." He is not understanding how difficult it is for these kids to concentrate on test scores when they have to work to help put food on the table. But when it comes to children that it (No Child Left Behind) was really meant for, urban children of poverty, it left these children behind. Urban centers are hit the worst. Their needs were not met. The government was not interested in their needs. Because the issues were not addressed in

the community, they could not focus on a test. And as it turns out, the test is all that matters. Now more and more of the kids are leaving. So, the closure of the district has not helped at all. When we were teaching at the high school, we would fundraise to take the kids on trips overseas, to see different cultures and countries. We cared deeply about these kids. We were invested in the kids. To be done the way we were, I feel that the State of Texas raped us. They took away our culture and our history.

Participant 13 (Group 2) said:

I did feel the pressure of passing the test, but I did not really know about how bad things had become in the district or with the schools I attended. I took AP classes, all the ones we offered, that is. We only had English and History AP classes. I had very good teachers, especially in the AP classes. I felt like I was well-prepared for college. I did become more aware of the problems when TEA came in to run the school. I was very disappointed that the district was closed. You see, I don't have any of my schools open anymore. My elementary school is gone; my intermediate school is not there. My middle schools and my high school don't exist. I can't return to my school and go to a football game or watch the band. It is a complete erasure of my educational experience.

Emerging theme four: Charter schools.

Emerging very close to student issues is the intersection of charter schools with research question two dealing with parent perspectives.
Participant 2 (Group 2) said:

In public schools, wherever the students are in their education, that is where we have to begin our instruction. With charter schools they can take the best and the brightest, and the public school is left with the rest. This is what Yes Prep did when they came into the district in 2009. They had the flexibility to change their curriculum, hold the kids longer in the day, etc. Bill and Melinda Gates Foundation sent in money to help, and just recently they sent in $200,000 dollars to another district to help with charter schools in that area. Charter schools have the advantage of educating the best in the area they are in and get the dollars necessary to achieve their goals. But in the meantime, children are being left behind in the public school and penalized for not meeting standards.

Participant 4 (Group 2) stated:

There were charter schools opening up in the area. The charter schools were horrible. I know because I worked for one of them. The owners of one of them were indicted. The school was corrupt. They had children on their books that were not at the school. Another charter I worked at was also corrupt. Very poorly run. That is when I left and came to the district that was recently closed.

Participant 9 (Group 1) said:

We found out that IDEA would be selecting their own faculty. Eastside teachers could reapply if they wished, but they would be selected in competition with other outside teachers applying to go to IDEA Allan and IDEA Eastside. IDEA Allan was open as a public charter school for one year. I know that families at Allan Elementary abandoned the concept of IDEA Allan. They left en masse.

Participant 7 (Group 1) stated:

Charter schools typically just serve the higher-performing kids since there is a selection of students made by the charter school, and they take the best and the brightest. This is not serving all the students. So essentially our tax dollars are going to support a private school with a public school district. This is unethical and immoral.

Participant 10 (Group 1) said:

> The principal, the CAC (Campus Advisory Council), the school board, Johns Hopkins are all there not really effecting any change. Everyone is talking but not doing. IDEA was brought in as a charter school. It failed because of the way it was handled at the beginning, and it shut out the parents. The charter school movement, from my vantage point, came in with seemingly good intentions, but it has changed. Now it is a business that is all about greed, and it's all about race. At the end of the day, it has to be about the public. If it is not about the public, then our democracy is at stake. If it is about corporate, then it is not about democracy. If democracy can't save democracy, then we won't have democracy.

Research question three. What are the perceptions of teachers and administrators who have been involved in the restructuring or school closure process?

Emerging theme one: AYP.

In research question three, two dominant themes emerged from the data. The first dealt with AYP issues. This was almost to be expected since educators in the schools are always focused on the percentages that are required each year to pass. The second dominant theme was concerning leadership failure. Adequate Yearly Progress issues are discussed first, with the participants giving testimony on what it was like to live through the closure process.

Participant 2 (Group 2) said:

> Has the closure of the district served the best interest of the children's education? I would say *yes* and *no* to that question. *Yes* is yet to be determined. It depends on how

the district that took our schools does with the children's education they took responsibility for. That district has demonstrated that they have had difficulty with the demographics in their own schools, which are similar to the demographics in our district. It remains to be seen what kind of job they will do with our students. They let go all of the employees, so they took responsibility with a whole new faculty and staff in all of our former schools. It left you scratching your head, wondering just what is the federal government trying to do here. How much privatization of education do they want? If the public schools are not meeting expectations because we keep having a moving target, are charter schools going to do better? If the district cannot afford the materials, technology, and added personnel, then how are you going to provide the necessary foundation to help the student be successful? It's one thing to say that no child will be left behind and that all children will pass the test by a certain date, but when the funds are not provided to help the schools in this effort, then that effort is bound to fail.

Participant 11 (Group 2) stated:

Teachers were offered big bonuses to come teach in our district after we were shut down. And now most of those teachers have quit because the system put in place is not getting the job done. We lost our entire school and our community when TEA shut us down. For what? We have teachers here from all over the country. They didn't know what they were walking into. Everything is now in disarray. These teachers brought in didn't have any connection or reason to stay. I also witnessed a lot of nepotism in the district. This did not help our situation. Friends and family were hired as teachers when they really were just substitutes. They stayed in the position when I think a real teacher could have been found.

Participant 3 (Group 2) said:

> They knew their jobs were on the line. At the first restructuring, they had a faculty meeting, and right there in front of everyone, the central administration said that all the core teachers would have to reapply for their jobs. And then they said that they were not concerned with the vocational teachers, and we could go ahead and leave the meeting. We knew it would not be easy to get teachers to come to our school district. Then the next year we had another restructure. This is when the two high schools were merged. We were told that we would get a fresh new start. Everyone would be starting over. That did not happen. In our minds, that meant that we would get a fresh start with the test accountability and with our evaluations. That did not happen. As vocational teachers, we also were worried about our jobs during the restructuring. We were told that our jobs could likely go to outside companies. Farm out the students and do away with the jobs. But first there were many programs shut down so that the budget could be worked to support academics that were part of the testing accountability. They shut down welding class; they shut down AC and Refrigeration. The band and choir suffered greatly because the funds were cut in these areas. They justified it by saying that the money was being diverted to academic needs. We were told to get over it when we inquired. We were told that this is the way it is and get used to it. In the end we did lose our jobs along with everyone else. Then our vocational building was torn down. Gone.

Emerging theme two: Leadership failure.

The constant turnover in principals led to a consistency of leadership being absent. This turnover was a result of the preceding principal not being able to achieve AYP standards. This was most prevalent in Group 2. In Group 1 leadership failure was seen to come from the central administration of the district.

Participant 1 (Group 2) said:

> The turnover problem had everything to do with the change in leadership every year. We lost the family atmosphere. People did not feel connected to the school anymore. This presented a real bad problem with teachers going the extra mile. Why should they? The turnover of the staff year-in and year-out is what contributed the most to the breakdown in the district. The test scores plummeted. Now the problems are so great it is going to be very hard to get the test scores up to par. After I left as principal, programs began to be cut due to a shortage of funds. They dropped the program that helped the most, the Dropout Prevention Program. That did not make sense, but they looked at all the programs and had to make decisions. They also closed the alternative school. That put more discipline problems back in the classroom.

Participant 12 (Group 2) said:

> It takes a principal at least two years to get his or her program established. You have to give him or her time. Same thing goes for the superintendent. I know there were five principals within a span of six years at the high school. It takes three years at least to see any kind of major change in a program. This was very bad judgment shown by the school board members at the time.

Participant 3 (Group 2) stated:

> Well, as I said, we never heard from the commissioner. We did not hear about it (closure) until we heard it on the news. That's when we heard that our jobs were gone.

There was no communication from the central office or our principal.

Participant 9 (Group 1) said:

Let me begin with Allan and how it came to be part of IDEA. The problem was with Eastside Memorial High School. It was IDEA's plan, which Austin ISD accepted, to create a vertical IDEA team. This is why it started with Allan. Allan was not failing in its accountability rating; they were acceptable. Now we are fractured, with no more Allan Elementary, and Eastside Memorial is still broken.

Participant 4 (Group 2) stated:

Now that the other district is in charge of our schools, they have more permanent subs there now than when we were there. They have brought in Teach for America teachers to help fill the spots. We were not allowed to use Teach for America teachers when we were still there. Now that they are in charge, they bring in Teach for America. That doesn't make sense. By Christmastime eight of the teachers had already quit. Even with a bonus they were given to sign up. More have quit since that time. Former teachers are not allowed on the property even at extracurricular activities like football games. The band program is not anything like it used to be. When the teachers were all replaced, it hit the kids hard. They came back to a school with all new teachers. None of the relationships were there that had been built up.

Research question four. What are the perceptions of parents of children affected through the restructuring of the neighborhood schools with regard to their representation in their taxation?

In this last research question, I was searching for intersections between the research question and other key emerging themes. The level of understanding the parents and educational professionals had about this topic amazed me. They understood what was at stake when a citizen's representation is compromised or completely removed. The following are what the participants reported coming out of emerging themes for research question four, representing charter schools, society issues, factors in test failure, and leadership failure. Due to so few indicators linking back to research question four, the emerging themes are addressed together as a group.

Participant 6 (Group 2) said:

> My taxes have been represented very poorly. The taxes we paid were not put back in the schools to run the programs that would keep the students in school. Right now we have no representation with the district that took us over. We don't have anyone we can call or write to that represents us in our community for our schools. The people they say represent us don't live in our community.

Participant 5 (Group 2) stated:

> The school district that took us over only wants the buildings and the land they are sitting on so they can get the tax dollars. They want the land. First of all, the number of school buildings being demolished: I question that, especially the vocational building being destroyed. We even had a community garden over there. We had a medical program there. We had a dental program.

Participant 8 (Group 1) said:

> At first we were very upset and unorganized, and I would say our tax dollars were not being used appropriately. Then we got organized and were able to begin making a difference. So now, we have a better chance of being represented because we replaced three board members through our efforts with the voters.

Participant 11 (Group 2) said:

Many parents who have relatives in other districts are trying to use them to get their children out of the district. This is just going to lower the enrollments even more. Rumors are flying now about what is really going on. Lots of talk about folks wanting the land. I know there are plans for expansion of roads. Right after the new district came in, property values went up. This means more taxes for them. Again, greed and money. I know this: we don't have any more board members. We pay our school taxes, but we don't have any school board members. No Child Left Behind has left our children behind. That's what I feel. We were like family. We didn't have a lot of resources, so we found ways to make it work and get the money raised for what we needed. But eventually it caught up to us.

Participant 7 (Group 1) stated:

Tax dollars are being used properly when they are being used to serve all students appropriately.

When research question four was asked of the education professionals, these responses added to the depth of the question.

Participant 1 (Group 2) said:

Since being taken over by the larger district, the community feels like they have lost all their representation. We used to have stakeholder meetings to brainstorm what needed to be done and who needed help. Now we have no representation. We used to have a school board to go to for complaints and suggestions. Even though they had problems, at least they were our people. Now with the closure, we have lost all of that.

Participant 3 (Group 2) stated:

> It makes me sick. When the district shut down, we lost our voice. The people who live in the area now have no knowledge of who their school board members are. In fact, we have no elected school board members now. We pay taxes but can't elect board members that represent us. Yes, that is exactly what it is. It is taxation without representation. I really feel overall that we got a raw deal.

Summary of Findings

In this chapter, the perceptions, opinions, and perspectives were presented from testimony through interviews from purposely selected participants.

Participants for interviews were selected first from surveys returned to the researcher and later from recommendations from those who had previously been interviewed. Creswell (2007) refers to this type of sampling as snowball or chain sampling. Criterion sampling was also used for selection of participants. The criterion required was their participation in a restructuring or closure event of a public school. This researcher then took the recorded interviews and transcribed them into a computer software analysis program titled QSR NVivo 10. Using the NVivo software, this researcher was able to create common topics spoken of by the participants when they answered the questions presented to them by this researcher. From the topics came emerging themes that intersected with the research questions in what is termed a matrix coding query. When the testimony from the participants was examined related to emerging themes intersecting with the research questions, the necessary data to draw conclusions were produced.

Searching for additional participants ended after Participant 13. The data were varied and represented triangulation with various demographic data represented. The data came, however, to saturation level, with no clear new information, or conflicting information, revealed through the participants' testimony. Saturation of the data occurs (Creswell, 2007) when new information that adds to understanding ceases to come forward.

The data presented a clear picture of the devastating impact No Child Left Behind policies and mandates have on children, parents and personnel in the schools. The increasing demands on meeting standards due to AYP percentages rising each year was seen by both parents and education professionals as the leading cause for their schools restructuring or eventual closure.

CHAPTER 5

Conclusions and Recommendations for the Future

In chapter 5 conclusions are drawn using data from testimony of participants and their relation to the research questions. Again, I will state for the reader that much of chapter 5 continues with the research findings from my dissertation. It is important for the sake of documentation that segments of the research are kept intact so that the reader can understand why conclusions were drawn in the manner stated. For the sake of clarification, it is helpful to understand why a qualitative study was chosen for the basic methodology.

This was a study about people and their issues in the schools. This was a study that required more than surveys that could be crunched into numbers for a measured finding, such as in a quantitative study. In a qualitative study, the participants in the study test the researcher's hypothesis through their responses to the research questions. Logic and reasoning are needed to draw conclusions after all the data are analyzed. The answers are not found in a statistical program. In a qualitative study, the answers to the research questions come from the logic and reasoning derived from the participant responses. Can I prove that No Child Left Behind was a policy written to intentionally drive schools to failure so that another method of education would emerge? Or can I state that logic and reasoning bear witness that NCLB was written with malice of intent to change the landscape of public education for the betterment of business interests and political gain and to bring about a new form of education?

This is important to keep in mind as the reader examines the information contained in chapter 5. Another important point to remember, this information was accumulated and written *prior to the 2014 deadline* that required schools to produce the 100% proficiency requirement.

Before any conclusions are given related to the research questions, the statement of the problem and purpose of the study are reviewed as taken from my dissertation. By reviewing the problem and the purpose of the study, information is fresh in the mind as the conclusions are drawn from the data.

Statement of the Problem

A crisis of failure is currently sweeping the public schools across the country. Schools are failing–not because students aren't learning academics or excelling in the arts, music, or vocational trades, but because the schools are not meeting a standard required of them by the state and federally mandated accountability standards.

Some schools have reached the maximum number of years that a school has to solve its testing outcomes and are now under restructuring measures by the state education agency. One option, written into NCLB policy, is to restructure the school into a public charter school. When this happens (Whittaker, 2012), the traditional concept of the neighborhood school is lost. As the percentages for proficiency increase for schools and school districts and the 2014 date gets closer, states are looking at an offer from the U.S. Department of Education. The waiver option from the Department of Education and President Obama allows states to avoid the 100% proficiency mandate but requires that they adopt new curriculum standards. School districts are faced with accepting the stipulations placed in the waiver or failing to meet the 2014 mandate that requires all students be proficient on the state-mandated test and federal-mandated Adequate Yearly Progress requirements.

Purpose of the Study

The purpose of this study was twofold. The first purpose was to present a grounded theory that describes the perceptions of the parents, teachers, and administrators located in two geographical locations. Each group shared the common denominator of school failure due to AYP non-compliance. One group was located in a diverse community located on the east side of an urban city in Central Texas. The other group was located on the north side of an urban city in Southeast Texas. The study highlighted the perceptions of the parents and educators impacted by the restructuring of the neighborhood schools and their perceptions of the No Child Left Behind (NCLB) policies that affected their families, their profession, and the communities. The second purpose of the study was to bring clarity to the beneficiaries of NCLB mandates that drive education policies. The study sought to determine who benefits from the federal AYP and the state accountability system and who their victims are. From the research in the literature and the dual purpose of the study, a theory was presented that sought to explain the intent of NCLB and demonstrate its impact on parents and the education profession. Clarity and understanding unfolded through this study that will serve to aid parents and the education professionals who seek to bring changes in education policy.

Conclusions of the Findings

Research question one. From the evidence presented, have the No Child Left Behind mandates served to propel schools and school districts toward AYP noncompliance?

This question was directly stated to each education professional as one of the interview questions. In the Interview Protocols for Education Professionals, they were asked in question six: "Please explain if you feel the accountability system in Texas and the federal Adequate Yearly Progress (AYP) standards have served to move schools to noncompliance and school failure."

Comments such as this one from Participant 2 were consistent with perceptions of other interviewed participants who were education professionals.

Participant 2 (Group 2) stated:

> One of the main things affecting the district dealt with No Child Left Behind dictating mandates that were unfunded by the federal government. All the ancillary

issues that were needed to bring students up to the levels that were dictated by the policy were left to the local districts to acquire. This put a huge strain on the local budgets. And this year, 2013–2014, we are expected to be 100%. What the general public doesn't understand is that you can't compare business standards and school education standards. With business if you get a defective product, you can send it back. You can't do that with a child. You have to work with what you get. Have the accountability system in Texas and the federal AYP standards served to move schools to non-compliance and school failure? With the way the system is set up, I would agree with that statement. Because the percentages to meet standards is a moving target and continually rising, and the funding is not provided to achieve the expectations, the groups that needed the extra help could not get the help they needed. The gaps were too wide, and with percentages to meet standards going up each year, it became an insurmountable mountain to climb. Add to this the cultural and societal issues that exist in areas of poverty, with both parents working and not at home, and many of the kids having to work when they get out of school every day, and the problems mount; No Child Left Behind does not address those issues. All it is concerned with is a test score. Education should develop the mind and spirit to make it in life. If the powers that be really wanted those things to happen, the money would have been provided to allow the school to do its job. The fact that the funds were withheld points to the fact that the powers that be did not want No Child Left Behind to succeed. And putting a percentage requirement of 100% by 2014 only confirms that they did not want it to succeed and schools were doomed to failure. The federal government made into law what outcome they wanted but failed to provide the necessary means to achieve the intended outcome. Also one has to recognize that when the system went from TAAS to TAKS, a much more difficult test was given to the students. This was the same time that AYP was introduced and the 2014 mandate was established. All of these factors contributed to the challenge placed upon schools and school districts and made the challenge of meeting standards impossible to achieve.

Each educational professional participant stated positively that he or she believed the way the policy of No Child Left Behind was written and implemented, there could be no other conclusion drawn except that it was a policy written to drive schools and school districts to noncompliance and eventual failure. These conclusions were drawn, again from the participants' testimony, due to the AYP percentages that year after year increased, moving schools toward the 100% proficiency on the test by 2014. There were large numbers of intersections in the matrix coding of emerging themes under question one with AYP (40), Factors in test failure (17), Leadership failure (17), and Student Issues (16).

The fact that schools were failing in record numbers, as is pointed out in the literature review of this study, did not cause the federal government and Department of Education to review the policy and give schools relief from penalties and sanctions. The resulting policy had devastating effects on those who were unable to meet the demands of the gradually increasing AYP percentages. The educators who were directly affected by these mandates and policies and had to endure the sanctions and penalties that resulted from AYP failure clearly understood why the sanctions and penalties were taking place. It was not because the teachers, counselors, and administrators were not doing everything they could think of to help the students and elevate the passing percentages. It was because the percentages written into the policy were unrealistic and placed in every school's path to accountability an obstacle that could not be overcome, especially in urban centers where societal inequities were the greatest.

This question was not asked of the parents involved in the two groups since the provisions that define AYP are not as clear to them as they are to the teachers and administrators. Parents did, however, understand that the reason for the restructure or closure of their schools was due to the mandates and policies of No Child Left Behind. This is examined in research question two.

Research question two. What are the perceptions of parents toward the restructuring or closure of their neighborhood schools?

Parents were asked the following two questions that relate to this research question.

Question five of the Interview Protocol for Parents asked: "What is your understanding of the No Child Left Behind mandates for schools and how they have affected your child's education?"

Question six of the Interview Protocol for Parents asked: "Is it your perception that No Child Left Behind has worked for the betterment of children and their education?"

Both of these questions gave insight into research question two. Four emergent themes dominated the intersections with research question two: Leadership failure (31), AYP (18), Student issues (12), and Charter schools (11). Parents saw leadership failure as central to the issues that led to their children's schools being affected by restructuring and closure.

Comments such as this one from Participant 5 (Group 2) were typical:

> In one day every person who worked in the district lost their job. They were out of work. Some still don't have work today. How do the people who did this sleep at night? They are not just hurting the adults; they are hurting the children. They want this land.

And this statement from Participant 9 (Group 1):

> As I said, the school district administration did not include us until it was a done deal and we became very vocal and began attending school board meetings. Now they really pay attention to us.

It was clear that the parents faulted leadership in the way the restructure issues were addressed with them.

AYP issues were referred to more as accountability, with comments such as this from Participant 9 (Group 1):

Oh, yeah. Absolutely, No Child Left Behind has definitely affected their education. Especially with the teachers and how they teach their class now ... Testing and accountability is pervasive. It is always there in every conversation with a teacher.

Or this comment from Participant 8 (Group 1):

I'm going to say no, No Child Left Behind has not worked for the betterment of children and the schools. The original plan and name sounded good to people. We were not going to leave children behind. The outcome of the plan has not worked out for the betterment of the children.

Student issues contributed in intersections with research question two, as evidenced by these participants' comments.

Participant 5 (Group 2) said:

Everyone learns on different levels. The old way of teaching was different levels. No Child Left Behind doesn't allow for different levels. This test asks questions that our kids know nothing about. Maybe some kids in richer districts, but not our kids. It has been a detriment to our children.

Participant 9 (Group 1) stated:

My fifth grader does well and does not struggle with the test. But last year when she was in the fourth grade was the first year that I became aware of how stressed-out she was about the test. She had it in her mind that if she did not do well on the test, she would not move on to the next grade. She was in tears about the testing environment in the testing area in the room.

Finally in intersections for research question two, Charter schools received 11 intersections. Again, parents saw the connection with No Child Left Behind and the testing accountability issues.

Participant 8 (Group 1) said:

> I believe the No Child Left Behind law in theory was a worthwhile proposal. But it has turned into a monster. It opened up the possibility of taxpayer-funded charter schools ... In October, at a meeting with the school and community, the superintendent announced to a shocked audience that they were bringing in a charter company named IDEA to take over the vertical team (of the high school).

Participant 7 (Group 1) added:

> I believe the contributing factors centered around the high school that was in the vertical team that included my child's elementary school. They were academically unacceptable for seven years. As a result, the high school was repurposed and renamed from Johnston High School to Eastside Memorial High School. There were also changes in leadership made by the school district. After this effort, the high school continued to fail to meet AYP standards, so the school district went through a process of reconstituting the high school and hired an outside entity to guide and direct the curriculum efforts of the school.

It was evident from the testimony of the parents that they viewed the restructuring of their neighborhood school as a very negative development. They also saw the connection with No Child Left Behind policies and mandates related to AYP and accountability. Failure of leadership played a dominant role in their perceptions and resulted in bitterness toward the school district and the State of Texas Department of Education. What is central to remember in all of these strong statements is that none of the restructuring or closures would have been necessary had it not been for

No Child Left Behind policies and mandates and the standards that the policies put in place for schools to attempt to find compliance.

> **Research question three.** What are the perceptions of teachers and administrators who have been involved in the restructuring or school closure process?

By asking research question three to the education professionals, it became very clear how they felt and how they perceived the issue of restructuring. This testimony was important because the education professionals in North Forest ISD not only went through restructuring, but they also advanced to the final stage of No Child Left Behind, which is closure. Due to the closure of the school district, these hardworking professionals who had devoted years to trying to solve the issues of accountability with their students, lost their jobs.

Participant 4 (Group 2) said:

> Now that the other district is in charge of our schools, they have more permanent subs there now than when we were there. They have brought in Teach for America teachers to help fill the spots. We were not allowed to use Teach for America teachers when we were still there. Now that they are in charge, they bring in Teach for America. That doesn't make sense. By Christmastime eight of the teachers had already quit. Even with a bonus they were given to sign up. More have quit since that time. Former teachers are not allowed on the property even at extracurricular activities like football games. The band program is not anything like it used to be. When the teachers were all replaced, it hit the kids hard. They came back to a school with all new teachers. None of the relationships were there that had been built up.

Participant 2 (Group 2) stated:

> Has the closure of the district served the best interest of the children's education? I would say *yes* and *no* to that

question. *Yes* is yet to be determined. It depends on how the district that took our schools does with the children's education they took responsibility for. That district has demonstrated that they have had difficulty with the demographics in their own schools, which are similar to the demographics in our district. It remains to be seen what kind of job they will do with our students. They let go all of the employees, so they took responsibility with a whole new faculty and staff in all of our former schools. It left you scratching your head, wondering just what is the federal government trying to do here. How much privatization of education do they want? If the public schools are not meeting expectations because we keep having a moving target, are charter schools going to do better? If the district cannot afford the materials, technology, and added personnel, then how are you going to provide the necessary foundation to help the student be successful? It's one thing to say that no child will be left behind and that all children will pass the test by a certain date, but when the funds are not provided to help the schools in this effort, then that effort is bound to fail.

Participant 3 (Group 2) said:

They knew their jobs were on the line. At the first restructuring, they had a faculty meeting, and right there in front of everyone, the central administration said that all the core teachers would have to reapply for their jobs. And then they said that they were not concerned with the vocational teachers, and we could go ahead and leave the meeting. We knew it would not be easy to get teachers to come to our school district. Then the next year we had another restructure. This is when the two high schools were merged. We were told that we would get a fresh new start. Everyone would be starting over. That did not happen. In our minds, that meant that we would get a fresh start with the test accountability and with our evaluations. That did not happen. As vocational teachers, we also were worried about our jobs during the restructuring. We were told that our jobs could likely go to outside companies. Farm out the students and do away with the jobs. But first there were many programs shut down so that the budget could be worked to support academics that were part of the testing accountability. They shut down welding class; they shut down AC and Refrigeration. The band and choir suffered greatly because the funds were cut in these areas. They justified it by saying that the money was being diverted to academic needs. We were told to get over it when we inquired. We were told that this is the way it is and get used to it. In the end we did lose our jobs along with everyone else. Then our vocational building was torn down. Gone.

Research question three was only asked to Group 2. The responses given were clearly delineated by the participants who lived the experience and were subjected to the final stage of No Child Left Behind. Education professionals were only included for Group 2. To restate, Austin ISD denied this researcher access to education professionals, which would have been part of Group 1. Group 2 education professionals saw the closure of their school district and the loss of their jobs. The effects on the education professionals, the parents, and the students were devastating. When one looks at the aftermath of this decision to close the entire school district, which came directly from the State of Texas, one can see the weight of the consequences from sanctions and penalties delivered to the schools and communities. This was all a result of the standards set in place by No Child Left Behind policy and mandates.

Research question four. What are the perceptions of parents of children affected through the restructuring of the neighborhood schools with regard to their representation in their taxation?

As stated previously, the level of understanding the parents and education professionals had about this question was very astute. The question was searching for beliefs about proper representation of their tax dollars and the threat of falling victim to taxation without representation. The following statements reveal that the participants had an understanding of the weight and magnitude of this question. The first statements were from parents.

Participant 6 (Group 2) said:

> My taxes have been represented very poorly. The taxes we paid were not put back in the schools to run the programs that would keep the students in school. Right now we have no representation with the district that took us over. We don't have anyone we can call or write to that represents us in our community for our schools. The people they say represent us don't live in our community.

Participant 5 (Group 2) stated:

> The school district that took us over only wants the buildings and the land they are sitting on so they can get the tax dollars. They want the land. First of all, the number of school buildings being demolished: I question that, especially the vocational building being destroyed. We even had a community garden over there. We had a medical program there. We had a dental program.

Participant 8 (Group 1) added:

> At first we were very upset and unorganized, and I would say our tax dollars were not being used appropriately. Then we got organized and were able to begin making a difference. So now, we have a better chance of being represented because we replaced three board members through our efforts with the voters.

Participant 11 (Group 2) said:

> I know this: we don't have any more board members. We pay our school taxes, but we don't have any school

board members. No Child Left Behind has left our children behind. That's what I feel. We were like family. We didn't have a lot of resources, so we found ways to make it work and get the money raised for what we needed. But eventually it caught up to us.

Research question four was also asked to the education professionals to get their perspective. Keep in mind that not all the education professionals interviewed lived in the school district where they worked. Most did, but not all. It would not be their personal tax dollars affected or their representation on the school board, but I felt it worthy to gain more depth to the question. In order to remain consistent with the parents' comments, the statements below are from education professionals who worked and lived in the school district that was closed.

Participant 1 (Group 2) said:

> Since being taken over by the larger district, the community feels like they have lost all their representation. We used to have stakeholder meetings to brainstorm what needed to be done and who needed help. Now we have no representation. We used to have a school board to go to for complaints and suggestions. Even though they had problems, at least they were our people. Now with the closure, we have lost all of that.

Participant 3 (Group 2) added:

> It makes me sick. When the district shut down, we lost our voice. The people who live in the area now have no knowledge of who their school board members are. In fact, we have no elected school board members now. We pay taxes but can't elect board members that represent us. Yes, that is exactly what it is. It is taxation without representation. I really feel overall that we got a raw deal.

The parents who contributed to research question four understood and believed that there was an issue with taxation when restructuring of a school, or worse, the closure of a school, takes place. The entity that is brought in to manage and operate the school, if it is a charter-school operation, is not answerable to a parent. They do not serve the taxpayer. They serve their stakeholders in the corporation that owns the charter school. When this happens, parents lose their representation with their tax dollars. This is a central point in this country's democratic form of government.

Summary of Research Questions

From the testimony given to the research questions by the participants, it is reasonable to conclude that the restructuring process or the closure of a school had a devastating impact on parents, students, education professionals, and the community. The effects were life changing for those who had to endure the process. In light of the participants' statements of beliefs from firsthand experience and taking into account the evidence from the research brought forth in the literature review of this dissertation, the following are conclusions drawn to the research questions.

Research question one. Participants' responses to the protocol questions relating to research question one provided evidence to the affirmative that No Child Left Behind mandates serve to propel schools and school districts toward noncompliance. The rise in AYP percentages needed to comply with standards grew to an unreachable percentage number and drove most every school in the country to AYP failure. The fact that the 100% requirement for student proficiency was placed into law through No Child Left Behind policy assured the eventual failure of almost every public school.

Research question two. Participants' responses to the protocol questions related to research question two provided evidence that the process of restructure or closure of a neighborhood school was very destructive to the lives of those who experienced the restructure or closure. The leadership of those who had authority over the process was fundamental in this process. As the participants' testimony points out, effective, sensitive, and empathic leadership was lacking from those who were in positions of leadership in the schools and school district affected. Some of the parents believed that ulterior motives were at play in the restructuring process. While these allegations are not provable, these beliefs gave rise to the distrust evident in the parents toward those in leadership positions in the schools and the community. A direct result of living through the restructuring and closure process of a neighborhood school was profound distrust of the leaders who acted in positions of authority. This was a most unfortunate consequence of the far-reaching elements of No Child Left Behind law.

Research question three. Professional educators who participated with their testimony provided evidence that working in a school that was under sanctions and threats from the state was a toxic environment to endure in a person's job. By and large, most educators are caring, diligent, and devoted individuals. They work hard every day to try to make a difference in a child's life. For many children these educators, whether teachers, counselors, or administrators, were sometimes the best hope they had for a bright future. This positive attitude and dedicated work ethic was clearly identifiable in the testimony from the education professionals' responses to the protocols established in the interview questions. Regarding the state accountability system and the federal AYP standards, the testimony of the participants clearly demonstrated that school personnel were working in an unwinnable situation in their attempt at meeting standards, whether state or federal. For the education professionals trapped in this matrix of accountability, facing this reality was untenable and incomprehensible.

Research question four. Evidence presented of parents' perceptions of their representation through their school taxes was cause for concern. From the parents' testimony and from the testimony of educators who worked in the district that was closed, the belief they were not being represented with their tax dollars was well established. The statements provided indicated that the concern of taxation without representation was reality to those participants. The helplessness exhibited by the people interviewed about the situation of no representation was also a grave concern. When public officials act in ways that are contrary to the liberties provided to the people in the Constitution, everyone's freedoms are threatened. The right of parents to govern the education of their children through public school board members that they elect is fundamental to the ability of parents to control how their public schools are operated. Take that right away, and the freedoms the people of this nation have enjoyed for years are jeopardized. No Child Left Behind policy and law give the rights of the people over to the rights of the state. The federal government has taken control of the education of the children through the establishment of *standards*, which establish *accountability*, thereby forcing teachers to focus on the testing outcomes of their students on the *assessment* so that their *appraisal* is not affected negatively, which has ended with *total control* of the system in the hands of the federal government.

Implications: A Closer Look at Standards

Reviewing that last sentence is worthwhile. *Standards* lead to an *accountability rating*, which is established by the *assessment*. Due to the impact of sanctions on the school from a poor accountability rating, teachers are now *appraised* according to the outcomes of their students on the test. This locks the teacher into a curriculum controlled through the essential elements that reflect the curriculum standards that gain an unnatural weight of value since these are the essential elements seen on the test. The system is *totally controlled* and teachers feel trapped, unable to fight for change or teach in a manner they see as effective since their evaluation is at stake.

Standards is a term that people have come to expect from just about every business, industry, and profession. People from the business world or legal profession are very comfortable with standards. Standards are expected. When standards are applied, however, to educating a young mind, they take on a different connotation. While standards are sometimes equated to quality or good performance, standards can also bring limitations. For an example: *The parameters of the standards will be limited to X.* Another example: *The standards for the information related to this topic will be derived from Y.* Those who control the standards control the knowledge allowed and where the knowledge is derived from. *Standards* in this case refer to a curriculum set of standards reflected through the essential elements of instruction. Standards for an accountability rating, however, are derived from something completely different. The accountability-rating standard comes from the outcomes of the subgroups as measured individually to judge whether a school is acceptable or a failure. The net result is that government has control over a school's success or failure and it has control over what is taught by the teacher. Only that which is tested can be taught, and any school that has one subgroup not meet standards is judged a failure.

How often has it been said that if only schools operated more like a business they would work more efficiently? That statement has been made so many times it has almost become an axiom in the school buildings all across America. Sound fiscal management is always appropriate, no matter what the setting. Strong ethical principles in dealing with human resource issues are applicable in every workplace situation. An argument could be made, however, that the education of a child is different. Confine it or limit it to a set of predetermined standards, and the child has now been relocated to an education that is *finite* instead of *infinite*. Students are seen as a product that must meet standards. The student's brain now has parameters it must adhere to in order for management to be satisfied and the corporate stakeholders to approve.

It can therefore be said that from the information revealed in the literature and the testimony of the participants, it is postulated that the education system is now run by what could be termed a *business model,* which is governed by standards: AYP standards and essential elements standards. In this business model for education control, the *AYP standards* are linked to the student *assessment,* which is tied to the *appraisal* of the teacher, and this is translated to the *accountability system* for the school and school district. Using the business model, the entities of assessment, appraisal, and accountability are quantifiable. Corporations understand quantifiable standards and by using standards (AYP) that can be measured, control is established.

Very gradually, incrementally, the education system has morphed from the finest liberal arts education the world had to offer into a structured, outcomes-based, data-driven, accountability-measured delivery system that bears little resemblance to the education system of a generation ago. Standards lead to accountability that leads to control. Success or failure is measured through the outcomes. AYP standards establish parameters for intended outcomes. When the intended outcomes are not achieved, it is the accountability system that applies penalties. The penalties imposed by the accountability system elicit behaviors in those receiving the penalties. When the penalties are sufficient enough to impose fear of job loss or loss of sovereignty over the operations of your school, autonomy and sovereignty are lost. The outcomes that are measured on the test indicate whether a child has been educated adequately, not the grade earned by the student in a course taught by a knowledgeable teacher from his or her vast experience in the field aided by a quality, district-vetted and -approved curriculum. A generation ago it was a curriculum that met the expectations of the school community and taxpayers. Now the curriculum is determined as a one-size-fits-all curriculum approved by people who have never set foot in a public school classroom as an adult.

Each state's education system finds itself coerced into more control from the federal government as states opt for the waiver to No Child Left Behind mandates or accept a grant in the Race To The Top incentive program launched by the federal government to assist states with budget issues related to funding education. In each of these endeavors, the waiver or the grant, the trade-off for the states was to agree to adopt the Common Core State Standards and tie teachers' evaluations to the outcomes of their students on the test. In so doing, the states have now placed the curriculum for every public school district in their state under federal control. As of 2013 only Texas, Nebraska, Minnesota, Virginia, and Alaska had not adopted the Common Core Standards. Now each of these holdout states has submitted to the U.S. Department of Education their plan for accountability. Texas is now under the waiver. In 2015 Texas will unfold its new teacher appraisal system, which has a testing outcome as part of the final evaluation. It is being piloted now in various school districts throughout the state. Other holdout states are in the process of doing the same. The takeover of the public school system in America is now complete.

Review of the Grounded Theory

No Child Left Behind (NCLB) is a policy that intentionally moves schools, especially those in urban settings, to failure, with the intended outcome of forcing schools to adopt a new education curriculum for new outcomes. This theory was derived from the research embedded in the literature written on the mandates and policies of NCLB. This theory was also formulated from this researcher's experience in the field as a teacher, an assistant principal, and a principal in the State of Texas who observed and participated in the intense high-stakes testing format. The students of Texas (and all other states within their own testing programs) have been tested for 30 years only to see their scores take them further and further away from an acceptable standard as outlined by the U.S. Department of Education. No Child Left Behind brought all schools under AYP. The AYP mandates have driven schools further away from the goal of NCLB, not closer to the goal. The intense pressure of high-stakes testing has extracted a toll on the education profession that is immeasurable. The damage to the children, who have had their psyches threatened with failure year after year, has had incalculable consequences. Based on the research, an analysis of NCLB law, and inductive reasoning and logic, this researcher concludes that NCLB was, from its conception in the minds of its planners, designed to drive schools to failure so that a new system could be established that would support an entirely different approach to educating the youth of America.

This book reflects the research taken from my dissertation submitted and accepted for my PhD. This book also reveals the testimony of those who have lived the experience of the intended outcome for schools under No Child Left Behind. The research and testimony give credence to the grounded theory presented. Other students, parents, and education professionals across the country who have looked the endgame of No Child Left Behind in the face would likely agree with the grounded theory presented in this book.

The framework for this dissertation was the Hegelian dialectic, as discussed in chapters 2 and 3. To review, social planners and power brokers from every industry that seek to control outcomes have used the dialectic for centuries. The *thesis* is the problem, the *antithesis* is the reaction to the problem, and the *synthesis* is the solution to the problem that represents a fair compromise. As pointed out in chapter 3, the key to understanding the Hegelian dialectic is recognizing that the planners who created the problem work to manage the reaction and finally present the solution that was planned before the problem ever materialized. It should be no surprise that the dialectic has been used in the education system. To control the minds of children and direct the path of the next generation serves to continue the plans that were developed and presented many years ago. A freethinking, well-educated populace is dangerous to those that wish to control outcomes. Although it is unsettling and shocking to realize this has taken place, why should it be any surprise that this has occurred? In relationship to the standards-based accountability system, in traditional Hegelian dialectic fashion, those who created the standards and established the outcomes are also those who have managed the public reaction to an increasing problem of failing schools. They are also the same who have given the public the solution to a nation full of failing schools. The answer given is total control of the education system in every state. Control of the education system no longer rests in the hands of the states, the public school officials and their school boards, or the public taxpayers. It is those entities that control the standards-based accountability system that control the education system.

One more important area needs review. After the 2011–2012 school year, the U.S. Department of Education, working in conjunction with the Obama administration, put the accountability system on hold. At that time the required percentage to "meet standards" with AYP was 87% for all subgroups. By this time most states had taken the waiver and agreed to change to Common Core and have teacher and principal evaluations related to their outcomes on the state test. As stated, there were some holdout states that did not agree, at the time, to come on the bandwagon. Texas was one of those states. President Obama and Secretary Duncan agreed to put AYP on hold to allow the holdout states to have more time to submit their education plans to Washington. These plans were to lay out the strategy that would be used by each state to make their schools and school districts accountable and measure up to the goals of the original 2014 100% mandate. In other words, the 100% mandate did not go away.

Texas submitted its plan (Texas Education Agency, 2013d) in September 2013 through the Texas Education Agency and Commissioner Williams. Of interest are the two components required by the U.S. Department of Education of all states in order to receive the waiver: map out the plan to achieve 100% proficiency and tie the teachers' and principals' evaluation to the outcomes of the test. What was missing from the plan was Texas agreeing to adopt Common Core Standards. Texas did not agree to go on

Common Core like all the other states receiving the waiver. We will have to wait to see how this plays out in the future.

In typical semantic deception manner, Adequate Yearly Progress has been changed in Texas and is now called annual measurable objectives (AMOs). At the time of this writing (fall of 2014), the AMOs for all subgroups in Texas schools is 83%. Next school year (2015–16), the AMOs will be 87%. This will produce wide-scale failing of schools again, just as it did in 2011. By the school year 2019–2020 (Texas Education Agency, 2013d), the public schools of Texas will be expected to be perfect in their test scores—100% proficient. Keep in mind, when politicians, radio talk show hosts, or other pundits talk about failing schools and not meeting standards, it is these percentages that are causing them to fail. Can any school realistically expect to meet these standards? Since none can, isn't it reasonable to propose that these standards have another agenda behind them? The grounded theory proposed through this book becomes clearer when it is viewed in this manner. This is why the accountability system must be dismantled.

Recommendations

Reversing the business model of the accountability system that controls the education system will not be easy. If true reform is to have any chance of shaking off the control mechanisms currently in place, it will take the unified effort of those in the trenches of the public school districts throughout the county to stand up and refuse to continue to support the current system. Teachers, counselors, and superintendents must all speak in one voice, and the elected school board members must listen and support that voice. Parents must also speak in one voice and refuse to subject their children to this insane system of constant testing. Most importantly, students must speak in one voice. This is beginning to happen as students in various parts of the country are standing up and refusing to take the standardized test. School officials need to view this as good and not seek ways to penalize these protesting students. School officials should embrace the protest and join the chorus of those who refuse to be manipulated any further. When the government officials in each state hear this voice, an opportunity for new policy is possible. Congressional

Representatives in Washington DC must support their constituencies in their state for this effort to have any chance of success. If they don't, the populace should remove them from office at the earliest opportunity. This will take a knowledgeable and informed electorate.

The following suggestions are made to guide future action.

1. Reject the business model governing the accountability system. Only when this is achieved will it open up a channel to recover the profession. More research is needed into business interests, lobbyists, and non-governmental agencies (NGO) in education, and their controlling influence.

2. Bring back local control through elected school boards, which appoint dedicated superintendents committed to the cause of returning the education profession to its sensible place as the preeminent purveyor of instruction and knowledge.

3. Superintendents and principals are to bring back the noble profession of teaching by allowing teachers to return as the authority of instruction in the classroom. The teacher is the cornerstone of a sound education system. The damage done to the profession from years of scripted lesson plans and intense accountability measures is immeasurable.

4. Continue to search out and identify the best and brightest of the student population and encourage their development through advanced placement-style programs.

5. Fund the arts, music, and extracurricular activities that provide enrichment, enjoyment, and a reason for many students to come to school.

6. Fund and encourage a vibrant and diverse vocational program to offer more students an opportunity to channel their interests and skills in a direction that may offer more interest than traditional higher education pathways. Students need options as they mature into adulthood.

Final Thoughts

Cognitive dissonance has played a huge role in the minds of those in the education profession. To allow this type of controlled system to take over a profession every educator holds dear would never have been allowed had not educators rationalized away the dangers that were presenting themselves. As mentioned previously, educators from every walk of life must break out of the mind-set that the education profession is on the right path. It is not. Is it any wonder why so many well-meaning teachers leave the profession every year? Those teachers who are older and remember a time when teachers actually taught from a brain-based, experience-driven ability now find themselves totally frustrated only working for a pension. New teachers can't imagine what they have encountered with this high-stakes, penalty-induced pressure that is not what they imagined for the teaching profession. It is really up to everyone who cares about the future of this great profession to break free from the shackles and prison of this standards-based, data-driven accountability system. It is those who are entrenched in the day-to-day struggle that have to step back and reclaim the profession so that the future of teaching is not lost and students can once again receive a quality education through the traditional public schools.

EPILOGUE

"The goal of education is the advancement of knowledge and the dissemination of the truth." —John F. Kennedy, 35th president of the United States

"The technotronic era involves the gradual appearance of a more controlled society. Such a society would be dominated by an elite, unrestrained by traditional values (of Liberty). Soon it will be possible to assert almost continuous surveillance over every citizen and maintain up-to-date complete files containing even the most personal information about the citizen. These files will be subject to instantaneous retrieval by the authorities." —Zbigniew Brzezinski, author and national security advisor in the Carter administration, and founding member of the Trilateral Commission

"Who controls the past, controls the future. Who controls the present, controls the past." —George Orwell, author of *1984* and *Animal Farm*

"Co-existence on this tightly knit earth should be viewed as an existence not only without wars ... But also without (the government) telling us how to live, what to say, what to think, what to know, and what not to know." —Alexander Solzhenitsyn, author and Soviet dissident.

The question should be asked, why would a government want to control information and knowledge? Wouldn't our leaders want us to be as informed as we possibly could be? Isn't an informed populace a strong and independent populace? Isn't that good for the country? I think you obviously see where I am going with these statements. The truth is, a public that is exhausted from the demands of daily work, distracted through sports and entertainment, and subjected to continuous propaganda from the news channels is a public that is easily controlled. Add to this a tight grip on the publications of books, magazines, and newspapers; a controlled media, combined with a controlled education system through accountability, and the formula is complete for near total control of the masses ability to acquire truthful and unbiased information and knowledge.

We live in a paradoxical age. On the one hand, people have more information at their fingertips than they ever have had in known history. Search engines can give instantaneous facts and knowledge about any subject wished to explore by an individual. Yet we are more ignorant than ever about some of the most basic information that people generally knew one generation removed. The reason for this is revealed in the very reason why this generation should be the most enlightened of all generations— technology. Technology provides information, but it also can be used to limit information. In our nations' schools, students now learn through the curriculum embedded into the laptop computer or tablet. This curriculum is tied into a nationalized set of standards linked directly to the test given yearly to determine school ratings, teacher evaluations, and whether a student is progressing at a rate that leads to eventual graduation. Teachers who have at least 20 years of experience understand that much of what they used to teach is not present in the new curriculum. Information and knowledge are now restricted to the standards applied to the curriculum that is evaluated on the national test.

This book has hopefully shed light on the desperate straits our education system finds itself in. This book is not intended to bring change. It is intended to inform. Only individuals correctly informed and working together can drive change. The individuals who want to bring change in the system, however, need accurate information that is directed at the right target. While many people today are focusing on the Common Core State Standards as the primary focus of their anger, it must be realized that until the accountability system is changed, it does not matter what curriculum set of standards is placed in front of the teachers and students—nothing will change. Knowledge will continue to be contained within the parameters of the test.

Consolidation of Information and Knowledge

The purpose of this book has been to illuminate and reveal how the education system got in this horrible condition and the mechanism that was used to accomplish the objective. It was also to highlight those individuals who have felt the heavy hand of misguided policies. The powers that control information and knowledge (Lutz, 2012) today have collected 90% of American media into six corporations. The six powerful conglomerates that control information and knowledge are G.E., Viacom, Disney, Time Warner, News Corp., and CBS (Lutz, 2012). Add to the big six Bertelsmann AG, based in Germany, having a powerful hold on the publishing market, owning Random House and Doubleday. Include in the mix as well, the Hearst Corporation and its influence over newspapers and magazine ownership, and the control over our information are left in very few hands. While it is very true that major sources of information like Google, Microsoft, and Yahoo are not owned by these major six to eight information-controlling corporations, the majority of time spent by Americans engrossed in some form of media is owned by one of these mega-conglomerates.

Search engines on the Internet are, most likely, the last bastion of free information that is unhindered if only the individual knew which questions to ask or what topics to research. It remains to be seen how this major source of brain food will be restricted in the future. For those who wish to control information and knowledge, the Internet is a threat. This is a main reason why major news outlets seek to discredit the Internet as being unworthy as a source of intelligent information.

This book has focused primarily on the education system and the restrictions placed upon parents, teachers, principals, and superintendents through state and federal accountability systems. There are many problems facing our country today—the economy and devaluation of the dollar, health care, threats of terrorism (real or imagined), lack of border security, threat of pandemics, urban unrest, and a loss of trust in the political system. The education of future generations, however, is certainly one of the most pressing, if not the most pressing issue of our time. Our very existence as an independent and freethinking people is at stake. The task of regaining independent control of our schools is a formidable challenge. It perhaps cannot be accomplished in our lifetime. If, however, some unforeseen event unfolds that enables the controlling entities of this world to fall and the opportunity presents itself for rebuilding, perhaps this book will help to shed light on what to avoid and how to proceed. Until that time, each of us has a responsibility to be informed and aware so that our actions and decisions, when it comes to educating our youth, are just and right.

"Educate and inform the whole mass of the people ... They are the only sure reliance for the preservation of our liberty." —Thomas Jefferson, third president of the United States and author of the Declaration of Independence

REFERENCES

Allen, G. (1972). *None dare call it conspiracy*. San Pedro, CA: CSG and Associates.

AustInnovation. (2010). Pearson scores nearly $470 M deal to run TAKS testing program in Texas. *Wordpress*. Retrieved from http://austinnovation.wordpress.com/2010/06/24/pearson-taks/

Banchero, S., & Dolan, M. (2012). Michigan city outsources all of its schools. *The Wall Street Journal*. Retrieved from http://online.wsj.com/article/SB10000872396390443545504577565363559208238.html

Broad Foundation. (2012). *The Broad Foundations*. Retrieved from http://www.broadfoundation.org/about_foundations.html

Brown, K. (n.d.). The two faces of NCLB. *Intercultural Development Research Association*. Retrieved from http://www.idra.org/IDRA_Newsletter/January_2005/The_Two_Faces_of_NCLB/

Buckley, K., & Fisler, J. (2002). *A decade of charter schools: From theory to practice* (CPRE, Policy Brief rb 35-1). Graduate School of Education, University of Pennsylvania.

Burke, L. (2012). Lack of confidence in public schools at an all-time high. *Heritage: The Foundry*. Retrieved from http://blog.heritage.org/2012/06/21/lack-of-confidence-in-public-schools-at-an-all-time-high/

Cavanagh, S. (2013). Marketplace K-12: Tracking business trends and emerging models in education. *Education Week, Spotlight*. Retrieved from http://blogs.edweek.org/edweek/marketplacek12/2013/03/amplify_insight_wins_contract_from_common_core_testing_consortium.html

Center on Education Policy. (2010). Update with 2009–10 data and five year trends. How many schools have not made Adequate Yearly Progress? Key findings. *Center on Education Policy.* Retrieved from www.cepdc.org/cfcontent_file.cfm?Attachment=Usher

Center on Education Policy. (2011). NCLB/ESEA waiver watch. *Center on Education Policy.* Retrieved from http://www.cepdc.org/page.cfm?FloatingPageID=21

Center on Education Policy. (2012). Year two of implementing the common core state standards: State's progress and challenges. *Center on Education Policy.* Retrieved from www.cep-dc.org/displayDocument.cfm?DocumentID=391KoberRenter_Report_commonCore_1.25.12(1)

Cherry, K. (2012). Cognitive dissonance—psychology definition of the week. *About.com Education Psychology.* Retrieved from http://psychology.about.com/b/2012/09/07/cognitive-dissonance-psychology-definition-of-the-week.htm

Combs, S. (2002). Window on state government, ED 1. *Texas Comptroller of Public Accounts.* Retrieved from http://www.window.state.tx.us/etexas2003/ed01.html

Creswell, J. W. (2007). *Qualitative inquiry and research design: Choosing among five approaches* (2nd ed.). Thousand Oaks, CA: Sage Publications, Inc.

Davey, M. (2012). Teachers strike in Chicago tests mayor and union. *The New York Times, Education.* Retrieved from http://www.nytimes.com/2012/09/11/education/teacher-strike-begins-in-chicago-amid-signs-that-deal-isnt-close.html?pagewanted=all

Dillon, S. (2009). Large urban-suburban gap seen in graduation rates. *The New York Times.* Retrieved from http://www.nytimes.com/2009/04/22/education/22dropout.html?_r=0

Distefano, J. (2013). Wall St. likes Philly public-school closings. *Philly.com.* Retrieved from http://www.philly.com/philly/blogs/inq-phillydeals/198489421.html

European Graduate School. (n.d.). Georg Wilhelm Friedrich Hegel—Biography. *European Graduate School: Graduate and Postgraduate Studies.* Retrieved from http://www.egs.edu/library/georg-wilhelm-friedrich-hegel/biography/

Ferenstein, G. (2011). Will computers replace schoolteachers? *CNN Opinion*. Retrieved from http://articles.cnn.com/2011-06-09/opinion/ computers.replace.teachers_1 _schools-change-online-teachers-cash strapped-school-istricts?_s=PM:OPINION

Frieden, T. (2002). Supreme Court affirms school voucher program. *CNN, Justice*. Retrieved from http://articles.cnn.com/2002-06-27/justice/ scotus.school.vouchers_1_school-voucher-program-milwaukee-and-florida-parochial-school-tuition?_s=PM:LAW

Gass, J. (2012). Is the Department of Education violating federal law by policy directing standards, tests, and curricula? *Pioneer Institute; Public Research*. Retrieved from http://www.missourieducationwatchdog. com/2012/02/pioneer-institute-asks-is-us-department.html

Goertz, M. E. (n.d.). *The federal role in defining adequate yearly progress: The flexibility/accountability trade-off (CPRE)*. Graduate School of Education, University of Pennsylvania. Retrieved from http://www. cpre.org/sites/default/files/researchreport/808_cep01.pdf

Gurria, A. (2010). *Presentation of the PISA 2010 results. Programme for International Student Assessment*. Organization for Economic Co-Operation and Development (OECD). Retrieved from http://www. oecd.org/unitedstates/presentationofthepisa2010results.htm

Haney, W. (2001). *Revisiting the myth of the Texas miracle in education*. Lynch School of Education, Boston College. Retrieved from Revisiting TXMyth.pdf

Hentschke, G. C., Oschman, S., & Snell, L. (2003). Trends and best practices for education management organizations. *West Ed Policy Perspectives*. Retrieved from www.wested.org/online

International Test Scores. (n.d.). Poor U.S. test results tied to weak curriculum. *4Choice*. Retrieved from http://4brevard.com/choice/ international-test-scores.htm

Iserbyt, C. (1999). *The deliberate dumbing down of America*. Parkman, OH: Conscience Press.

Iserbyt, C. (2002). Death sentence for private and home education, courtesy of supreme court. *Free Republic*. Retrieved from http://www. freerepublic.com/focus/news/713173/posts

Iserbyt, C. (2011). *The deliberate dumbing down of America (Revised ed.)*. Parkman, OH: Conscience Press.

Iserbyt, C. (2012). Heritage Foundation, NAFTA: School choice and the destruction of traditional education. *News with Views*. Retrieved from http://www.newswithviews.com/iserbyt/iserbyt111.htm

Jennings, J. (2012). Why have we fallen short and where do we go from here? *Center on Education Policy*. Retrieved from www/cep-dc.org.

Kjos, B. (n.d.). *The mind changing dialectic process*. Retrieved from http://www.crossroad.to/articles2/Reinventing2.htm

Klein ISD News Release. (2011). Understanding Texas Public School Accountability *News Release Klein ISD*, August, 15, 2011. Retrieved from http://www.kleinisd.net/default.aspx?name=ezsearch

Klonsky, M. (2011). Common Core Curriculum—who's on board? Who's not? *Huffington Post.com*.

Retrieved from http://www.huffingtonpost.com/michael-klonsky-phd/common-core-curriculum_b_845364.html

Kumashiro, K. K. (2012). When billionaires become educational experts. *American Association of University Professors*. Retrieved from http://www.aaup.org/article/when-billionaires-become-educational-experts#.UZJ8m4IYK9Y

Leal, F. (2011). State: Obama testing waiver will cost $3.1 billion. *Orange County Register*. Retrieved from http://www.ocregister.com/news/state-325281-waiver-teacher.html

Lee, T. (2009). *The human fallout: Educator's perspectives about No Child Left Behind (NCLB) implementation in urban schools* (Doctoral dissertation). Retrieved from ProQuest Dissertation and Thesis. (UNI Number, 3363314).

Legal Information Institute. (2002). Zellman v. Simmons-Harris (00-1751) 536 U.S. 639 (2002) 234 F.3rd 945, reversed. *Cornell University Law School*. Retrieved from http://www.law.cornell.edu/supct/html/00-1751.ZS.html

Lodhia, P. (2013). North Forest ISD loses final appeal: Will close Monday. *ABC News Affiliate, KTRK, Channel 13*. Retrieved from http://abclocal.go.com/ktrk/story?section=news/local&id=9156050

Lutz, A. (2012). These 6 corporations control 90% of the media in America. *Business Insider*. Retrieved from http://www.businessinsider.com/these-6-corporations-control-90-of-the-media-in-america-2012-6

Manno, B. V. (1994). Outcome-based education: Has it become more affliction than cure? *Center of the American Experiment*. Retrieved from http://www.americanexperiment.org/publications/reports/outcome-based-education-has-it-become-more-affliction-than-cure

Mass, W. (2002). Taking the voucher bait (The last word). *Questia, Trusted Online Research*. Retrieved from http://www.questia.com/library/1G1-90402205/taking-the-voucher-bait-the-last-word

McCune, G. (2012). Chicago teachers end strike: School to resume Wednesday. *Reuters*. Retrieved from http://www.reuters.com/article/2012/09/18/us-usa-chicago-schools-idUSBRE88E0IV20120918

McLeod, S. (2007). Skinner: Operant conditioning. *Simply Psychology*. Retrieved from http://www.simplypsychology.org/operantconditioning.html#sthash.Ih72qrZJ.dpbs

McLeod, S. (2008). Cognitive dissonance. *Simply psychology*. Retrieved from http://www.simplypsychology.org/cognitive-dissonance.html.

McNeil, M. (2011). Are 82% of schools 'failing' under NCLB, as Duncan warned?
McGraw Hill, Politics K-12. Retrieved from http://blogs.edweek.org/edweek/campaign-k-12/2011/08/are_82_of_ schools_unde.html

McGraw Hill, Politics K–12. Retrieved from
http://blogs.edweek.org/edweek/campaign-k-12/2011/08/are_82_of_schools_unde.html

McNeil, M. (2013). Teacher-evaluation plans bedevil waiver states. *Education Week*.
Retrieved from
http://www.edweek.org/ew/articles/2013/03/06/23waivers_ep.h32.htm

Mead, S. (2007). Easy way out: "Restructure" usually means little has changed.
Education Next. Retrieved from http://educationnext.org/easy-way-out/

Mellon, E. (2013). Education rivals work together in spring branch. *The Houston Chronicle*. Retrieved from http://www.houstonchronicle.com/news/Houstontexas/houston/article/Spring-Branch-ISD-charter-schools-embrace-unity-4168879.php

Omer, S. (2012). Question at heart of Chicago strike: How do you measure teacher performance? *NBC News*. Retrieved from http://usnews.

nbcnews.com/ news/2012/09/11/13808109-question-at-heart-of chicag strike-how-do-you-measure-teacher-performance?lite

Orange, A. (2012). *"I don't care if the students are learning": A case study of implementation and interpretation in Virginia* (Doctoral dissertation). Retrieved from ProQuest Dissertation and Thesis. (UNI Number: 3530506).

Ott, A. (2010). *History of high stakes testing: A timeline of test in Texas.* Retrieved from https://classes.lt.unt.edu/Spring_2010/ CECS_5420_020/lao0041/Assign%203/index.html

Phillips, A. (2010). *Murdoch buys education tech company Wireless Generation.* Gotham Schools: Education Marketplace. Retrieved from http://gothamschools.org/2010/11/22/ murdoch-buys-education-tech-company-wireless-generation/

Popham, W. J. (1999). Why standardized tests don't measure educational quality. *ASCD, Educational Leadership.* Retrieved from http://www. ascd.org/publications/educational-leadership/mar99/vol56/num06/ Why-Standardized-Tests-Don%27t-Measure-Educational-Quality. aspx

Raapana, N., & Friedrich, N. (2005). *What is the Hegelian Dialectic?* Retrieved from http://www.crossroad.to/articles2/05/dialectic.htm

Raver, E. (2006). *A discussion of B. F. Skinner's revolutionary work, "Beyond Freedom and Dignity."* Retrieved from http://voices.yahoo.com/a-discussion-bf-skinners-revolutionary-work-beyond-76859.html

Ravitch, D. (2010). *The death and life of the great American school system: How testing and choice are undermining education* (Revised and expanded edition). New York, NY: Basic Books, Perseus Books Group.

Ravitch, D. (2011). School "reform": A failing grade. *The New York Review of Books.* Retrieved from http://www.nybooks.com/articles/ archives/2011/sep/29/school-reform-failing-grade/

Resmovits, J. (2012). *No Child Left Behind waivers granted to 33 States.* Retrieved from http://www.huffingtonpost.com/2012/07/19/no-childleft-behind-waiver_n_1684504.html

Riley, B. (2012). Waive to the top: The dangers of legislating education policy from the executive branch. *American Enterprise Institute.* Retrieved from http://www.aei.org/outlook/education/k-12/system-reform/

waive-to-the-top-the-dangers-of-legislating-education-policy-from-the-executive-branch/

Scott, C. (2008). A call to restructure restructuring: Lessons from the No Child Left Behind Act in five states. *Center on Education Policy.* Retrieved fromhttp://www.cep-dc.org/displayDocument. cfm?DocumentID=175

Silverthorn, D. U. (2006). Teaching and learning in the interactive classroom. *American Psychological Society.* Retrieved from http://advan. physiology.org/content/30/4/135.full

Stanford Encyclopedia of Philosophy. (2005). *Epistemology.* Retrieved from http://plato.stanford.edu/entries/epistemology/

Strauss, V. (2010). Why Obama, Duncan should read Linda Darling-Hammond's new education book. *The Washington Post: The Answer Sheet.* Retrieved from http://voices.washingtonpost.com/answer-sheet/ education-secretary-duncan/why-obama-duncan-should-read-l.html

Strauss, V. (2011). Darling-Hammond: The mess we are in. *The Washington Post: Post Local.* Retrieved from http://www.washingtonpost.com/blogs/ answer-sheet/post/darling-hammond-the-mess-we-are-in/2011/07/31/ gIQAXWSIoI_blog.html

Taylor, D. (2010). For KIPP charter schools, more computer time, less class time. *WordPress.com.* Retrieved from http://seattleeducation2010.wordpress.com /2012/12/26/ for-kipp-charter-schools-more-computer-time-less-class-time/

Texas Education Agency. (2011). *2011 Adequate Yearly Progress (AYP: AYP guide).* Retrieved from http://ritter.tea.state.tx.us/ayp/2011/

Texas Education Agency. (2012 a). AEIS campus report. Retrieved from http://ritter.tea.state.tx.us/perfreport/aeis/2012/index.htmletrieved from

Texas Education Agency. (2012 b). *2012 AYP on the rise.* Retrieved from http://www.tea.state.tx.us/index4.aspx?id=2147508195

Texas Education Agency. (2013 a). *Charter schools.* Retrieved from Texas Education Agency. (2013b). *School improvement grants.* Retrieved from http://www2.ed.gov/programs/sif/summary/tx.pdf

Texas Education Agency. (2013c). *Commissioner Williams recommends closure of North Forest ISD.* Retrieved from http://www.tea.state.tx.us/ news_release.aspx?id=2147512209

Texas Education Agency. (2013d). *Commissioner Williams: Texas secures conditional NCLB waiver.* Retrieved from http://www.tea.state.tx.us/index4.aspx?id=25769807569

Touhey, E. (2011). Education Secretary: "No Child Left Behind" has led to a "dumbing down." *The Hill's Congress Blog.* Retrieved from http://thehill.com/blogs/congress -blog/the-administration/140977-interview-with-education-secretary-arne-duncan

U.S. Department of Education. (n.d.)a. *Improving basic programs operated by local education agencies.* Retrieved from http://www2.ed.gov/legislation/ESEA/sec1111.html

U.S. Department of Education. (n.d.)b. *ESEA flexibility.* Retrieved from http://www2.ed.gov/policy/elsec/guid/esea-flexibility/index.html

Varghese, R. (2013). Closing 12% of Philadelphia schools creates winners: Muni.credit. *Bloomberg.com.* Retrieved from http://www.bloomberg.com/news/2013-03-06/closing-12-of-philadelphia-schools-creates-winners-muni-credit.html

Whittaker, R. (2012). Farewell to Allan. *The Austin Chronicle.* Retrieved from http://www.austinchronicle.com/news/2012-06-01/farewell-to-allan/all/

Wohlstetter, P., and Griffin, N. C. (1997). Charter schools as learning communities. *Graduate School of Education, University of Pennsylvania.* Retrieved from CPRE Policy Briefs RB-22-September, 1997

Woodward, B. A. (2011). *Amidst the test: The lived experience of teaching "under" No Child Left Behind.* (Doctoral dissertation). Retrieved from ProQuest Dissertations and Thesis. (UNI Number: 3495419).

Young, R., and Kelleher, J. B. (2013). In Chicago, thousands march to protest proposed school closings. *Reuters.* Retrieved from http://www.reuters.com/article/2013/03/28/us-usa-education-chicago-idUSBRE92Q1ER20130328